GUILT-FREE

NICE

CREAM

MARGIE BROADHEAD

GUILT-FREE

NICE

CREAM

OVER 70 AMAZING DAIRY-FREE ICE CREAMS

PHOTOGRAPHY BY JACQUI MELVILLE

hardie grant books

CONTENTS

INTRODUCTION

Nice Cream is one of the best things ever. Fact. But what exactly is nice cream, I hear you cry? Essentially it's a healthy, banana-based alternative to ice cream, which happens to also be delicious and super easy and quick to make. Using frozen bananas ensures a magically creamy and deliciously good-for-you frozen treat.

Nana Nice Cream was launched in the UK by Margie Broadhead, a professional chef and food blogger with a simple mission: to make great tasting food that actually does you good. This is shown by the fact that our pots of (ba)nana nice cream count as one of your five a day; they are dairy-free, have no preservatives and are completely natural. Bananas also happen to be ridiculously good for you. They are bursting with potassium, and full of energy.

Whilst our exact award-winning recipe remains a heavily guarded secret, the good news is there are lots of variations and nice cream is really fun to make at home. It is wonderfully simple to whip up. You don't require superhuman powers in the kitchen, nor do you need a fancy ice-cream maker or any specialist equipment. You just need to love bananas.

We at Nana Nice Cream like to think of ourselves as aficionados in the art of making nice cream, so we have put together some useful tips to guide you on your journey (pages 10–11).

One of the joys of nice cream is the sheer versatility. The flavour possibilities are endless, and you can really let your imagination run wild. We love it just as it is, straight from the blender, but we also love having it for breakfast in a smoothie bowl (pages 48–50) or scooped on top of pancakes (page 43). We love it as a post-gym snack whipped into a protein smoothie (page 51), or in the form of a refreshing ice-lolly on a hot day (pages 65–79). And, of course, we love it for pudding, drizzled with chocolate, layered between cakes or just licked off a spoon.

We hope you enjoy using this book as inspiration and, most of all, we hope you have fun with the recipes that follow.

LET'S TALK THE BASICS

There are two types of nice cream in this book. One is a soft-serve version, which you can whip up in an instant and enjoy straight away. The other is frozen and more akin to traditonal ice cream. It is whipped up in the same manner as the soft-serve version but then given a blast in the freezer to firm up so that you can scoop it (just as you would a regular ice cream).

Both versions are just as good and incredibly simple to make. Go with whichever you prefer for whatever the occasion. It's up to you to experiment and just have fun.

Use ripe bananas that are ideally at the stage just before they turn really spotty and overripe. It gives a better overall taste to nice creams, and they are a lot easier for your body to digest.

All the recipes in this book that list 'peeled and frozen' bananas assume they are prepared using the freezing method on the opposite page.

TRICKS OF THE TRADE

Our preferred tool of choice for blending the nice creams is a food processor. If you have a high-speed blender, this is also a good option. Of course, if you have an ice-cream maker, then by all means add your blended mix to the machine to chill it, while it whips a bit of extra air into it – this will no doubt make it even better – but please don't fret if you don't have one.

Have fun with the lollipops and all the moulds and sticks that you can get! But again, please don't worry if you don't have all the right equipment. Recycled yoghurt pots make great popsicle moulds, as do little jelly moulds, ice cube trays and loaf tins. As for lolly sticks, you don't need anything too specialised: staws, wooden forks and spoons work brilliantly. For something more fun (and edible) why not try liquorice or even pretzel sticks!

Although our completely healthy nice creams are amazing, it is important to remember that they aren't ice creams in the traditional sense and so need to be treated a little differently. Vegan ice creams in general require a bit more thawing than store-bought sugar-laden ice creams. This just means that the nice creams need to sit out of the freezer for about 15 minutes before serving. This will give them a chance to become lovely and scoopable.

It's also worth pointing out that nice creams are best if not left to wallow for too long in the freezer. This is something we have personally never found to be a problem as they are too delicious to be left for too long!

How to Freeze Bananas

To make nice cream, it is important to freeze the bananas first. I always keep a stash in the freezer, ready for whenever I need them! It is up to you how many bananas you want to freeze, but it is a great way to use up any that are starting to blacken and spot.

1. Peel the bananas and discard the skins.
2. Slice into 2.5–5 cm (1–2 in) chunks.
3. Arrange the bananas, in a single layer, on a baking tray lined with baking parchment and freeze for 2 hours or until frozen.
4. Transfer to Ziploc® bags until ready to use!

Basic 'Banilla' Soft-Serve Nice Cream

It is so easy and quick to tranform bananas into a deliciously creamy nice cream. This is my go-to method for a basic soft-serve nice cream, celebrating that gorgeous banana taste. Ideally, use 1–2 bananas per person.

Serves 1

1–2 large bananas, peeled and frozen
¼ tsp vanilla extract
a pinch of sea salt

1. Pop all the ingredients in a food processor and blend. At first, the bananas will resemble banana breadcrumbs – don't panic! Scrape down the sides of the food processor every 30 seconds, and keep blending.
2. Blend until it's really creamy and soft-serve-like in texture.
3. Serve immediately.

Basic 'Banilla' Frozen Nice Cream

If you want to make a scoopable frozen nice cream – more akin to a traditional ice cream – you will need to add a few more ingredients. Adding a source of sugar and some healthy fats will ensure your finished nice cream is deliciously creamy.

Serves 1

1–2 large bananas, peeled and frozen
¼ tsp vanilla extract
a pinch of sea salt
2 Medjool dates, pitted
2 tbsp coconut cream

1. Blend the bananas, vanilla extract and salt together in a food processor until smooth and creamy. Scrape down the sides of the food processor every 30 seconds, and keep blending.
2. Add the dates and coconut cream to the mixture and blend for a few more minutes until fully combined.
3. Transfer the mixture to a freezer-proof container and cover with cling film (plastic wrap) or a lid. Freeze for 3 hours, stirring every 30 minutes to prevent ice crystals from forming. Alternatively, pour this into an ice-cream maker and prepare according to the manufacturer's instructions.
4. Allow the nice cream to sit at room temperature for 15 minutes before scooping.

THE PERFECT DAIRY-FREE
NICE CREAM

The art of nice cream is actually more scientific than you might think. To stop your delicious creation freezing into a solid banana ice cube you need to add a balance of fats and sugars, but don't worry – there are lots of healthy fats and unrefined sugars available.

Here are some of our favourites:

FATS

Fats are critical in making sure your nice cream is thick and creamy. There are lots of healthy fats to choose from that can give your nice-cream creations a delicious and rich texture.

Avocado
Coconut milk* or coconut oil
Nuts or nut butters
Plant-based milks (almond, cashew, soy milks)
Raw cacao butter

* Use full-fat tinned coconut milk and keep it in the fridge overnight (to allow it to separate), then use the thick, white coconut cream that settles at the top. Save the watery coconut milk for another recipe or add to your morning smoothie.

SUGARS

At Nana Nice Cream HQ, we favour natural, fruit-based sweeteners over refined sugar. It's worth noting that liquid sweeteners tend to produce nice creams with the fewest ice crystals.

Agave syrup
Apple purée
Coconut nectar or coconut sugar
Date syrup or dates (we like Medjool dates)
Grape juice
Honey
Maple syrup
Pineapple juice

Like most good recipes, ours aren't prescriptive, so please don't stress if you don't have the exact ingredients to hand. Although we've tried to suggest alternatives, feel free to swap in and swap out as you like. If you aren't a fan of maple syrup, simply use coconut nectar or agave syrup instead. If you want to make your nice cream only with fruit, then play around with apple purée, grapes and dates. It's just a case of finding a balance, and what works for you. The process of making nice cream, like all the best things, is meant to be fun, so relax and enjoy.

▼▼▼▼▼▼▼▼▼▼▼▼

NICE
CREAM

▲▲▲▲▲▲▲▲▲▲▲▲▲▲

BANANA AND KIWI
NICE CREAM

Serves 1

2 bananas, peeled and frozen
1 fresh kiwi, peeled and chopped

Who would have thought that bananas and kiwi go together? Well they do. I love this tropical little combination.

Put the bananas in the food processor and blend until thick and creamy. Then add the kiwi and blend until combined, being careful not to over-blend otherwise the banana will become too soft. Enjoy straight away.

BANANA AND NUTELLA®
NICE CREAM

Serves 1

2 bananas, peeled and frozen • ½ tsp vanilla extract
85 g (3 oz/¼ cup) Nutella® or It's Not Nutella® Spread (page 130)

Banana and Nutella® are a match made in heaven. So simple, so good and so addictive!

Put the bananas in the food processor and blend until thick and creamy, scraping down the sides every 30 seconds. Process until the mixture becomes completely smooth and has the consistency of ice cream. Add the vanilla extract and Nutella®, then pulse until combined. Eat straight away.

Top Tip: You could swap the Nutella® for 1 tablespoon unsweetened cacao powder or cocoa powder and a little squirt of maple syrup.

CARAMELISED BANANA
NICE CREAM

✿

Serves 2

4 bananas • 1 tbsp coconut oil
2 tsp coconut sugar • pinch of salt
125 ml (4 fl oz) tinned coconut milk, chilled (thick part only)

✿

A really simple way to jazz up the nice cream is to caramelise the bananas first. These caramelised bananas are really easy to do, and are ridiculously delicious just as they are. If you can resist the temptation to eat them straight from the pan, they make an insanely good nice cream.

Slice 2 of the bananas and place the slices in a sealed bag or container in the freezer overnight, or for at least 8 hours. Slice the remaining 2 bananas into rounds at least 1 cm (½ in) thick.

Melt the coconut oil in a pan over medium-high heat and add the coconut sugar and salt. Place the banana slices in the pan. Cook until the bottoms turn golden brown and caramelised. Flip the slices over and brown on the other side.

Transfer the caramelised bananas along with any sticky juices to a container or thick Ziploc® bag, and freeze for 8 hours or overnight.

Place the frozen bananas (both caramelised and uncaramelised) in the food processor and blend until smooth. Scrape down the sides and add the coconut milk, then continue to blend until very smooth and has the consistency of soft-serve ice cream. Serve immediately.

VERY BERRY NICE CREAM

✽

Serves 1

2 bananas, peeled and frozen
110 g (4 oz/¾ cup) blackcurrants or blackberries
1 tsp vanilla extract • fresh sprig of mint (optional)

Wonderfully dramatic in colour and full of flavour – this will become one of your staples.

Put the bananas, berries, vanilla extract and mint leaves (if using) in the food processor and blend until thick and creamy, scraping down the sides every 30 seconds. Process until the mixture becomes completely smooth and has the consistency of soft-serve ice cream. Enjoy before it melts.

PEANUT BUTTER NICE CREAM

✽

Serves 1

2 bananas, peeled and frozen
85 g (3 oz/¼ cup) smooth peanut butter
½ tsp vanilla extract

Peanut butter and banana... the new peanut butter and jello! This is ridiculously tasty.

Put the bananas, peanut butter and vanilla extract in the food processor and blend until thick and creamy, scraping down the sides every 30 seconds. Process until the mixture becomes completely smooth and has the consistency of soft-serve ice cream. Serve immediately.

Top Tip: This is also incredible with an added ½ tablespoon of unsweetened cacao or cocoa powder or ½ tablespoon of chocolate chips.

STRAWBERRY AND RHUBARB CRUMBLE NICE CREAM

*

Serves 4

For the crumble:
100 g (3½ oz/1 cup) gluten-free oats • 150 g (5 oz/1 cup) almonds • 2 tbsp coconut oil
4 tbsp maple syrup • a pinch of ground ginger

For the stawberry and rhubarb nice cream:
2 big stalks rhubarb, cut into 1 cm (½ in) lengths
3 tbsp maple syrup • juice of ½ lemon • 3 bananas, peeled and frozen
160 g (5½ oz/1 cup) strawberries, fresh or frozen
400 ml (14 fl oz) tinned coconut milk, chilled (thick part only)
1 tbsp melted coconut oil • 1 tsp vanilla extract

*

Strawberries and rhubarb epitomise the beginning of summer and that's exactly how this lovely little recipe tastes; like summer in a bowl.

Preheat the oven to 190°C (375°F/Gas 5) and line a baking tray approximately 20 × 20 cm (8 × 8 in) with baking parchment.

First make the crumble topping. Place the oats and almonds in a food processor, and pulse until nice and crumbly. Heat the coconut oil, maple syrup and ginger in a small saucepan over a low heat. Add the liquid mix to the oats and almonds, and pulse in the food processor. Sprinkle the crumble evenly into the baking tray and bake for 10 minutes, then remove from the oven and leave to cool.

For the nice cream, toss the rhubarb with 1½ tablespoons of maple syrup and the lemon juice in a large, shallow baking dish. Cook the rhubarb in the oven for 20 minutes, until lovely and tender. When the rhubarb is completely tender, remove and let it cool a little before blitzing in a food processor. Add the frozen bananas and blend until thick and creamy, then add the remaining maple syrup plus the rest of the nice cream ingredients and blend again until smooth.

Stir in the cooled crumble mixture and scoop straight into bowls to serve, or for a firmer ice-cream consistency, pour in a freezer-proof container and freeze for 1 hour to firm up.

BANANA, RUM AND RAISIN NICE CREAM

✼

Serves 4

115 g (4 oz/¾ cup) raisins
5 tbsp rum (or more or less depending on how boozy you want it)
500 ml (17 fl oz) tinned coconut milk, chilled (thick part only) • 150 g (5 oz/¾ cup) coconut sugar
2 tbsp arrowroot powder • 3 bananas, peeled and frozen
1 tsp vanilla extract

✼

In our opinion, the only way a rum and raisin ice cream can be improved upon is by adding a good old punch of banana. Perfect for a dinner party as it's so easy to whip up, but don't worry, your guests don't have to know that...

Put the raisins in a small bowl and pour over 3 tablespoons rum. Leave to soak for 10 minutes.

Pop roughly three-quarters of the coconut milk in a saucepan and add the coconut sugar. Heat gently for a couple of minutes until the sugar has dissolved.

Mix the arrowroot powder and the remaining coconut milk together in a small bowl and then pour this into the saucepan. Continue to warm for another couple of minutes until the mixture becomes lovely and thick and coats the back of the spoon. Turn off the heat and leave to cool.

Once cool, add the mixture to a food processor along with the frozen bananas, vanilla extract and the remaining rum. Blend until thick and creamy. Stir in the rum-soaked raisins.

Pop the nice cream into a freezer-proof container and freeze for about 3 hours to firm up, stirring every 30 minutes to prevent ice crystals. Alternatively you can pour the mixture into an ice-cream maker and prepare according to the manufacturer's instructions.

VANILLA NICE CREAM WITH RASPBERRIES AND HONEY-ROASTED MACADAMIA NUT BUTTER SWIRL

✿

Serves 4

For the honey-roasted macadamia nut butter
(makes approx. 1 × 200 ml/7 fl oz jar):
2 tbsp honey • 4 tsp melted coconut oil
½ tsp ground cinnamon • a pinch of sea salt
200 g (7 oz/2 cups) raw whole macadamia nuts

For the nice cream:
4 bananas, peeled and frozen
400 ml (14 fl oz) tinned coconut milk, chilled (thick part only)
1 tsp vanilla extract • 125 g (4½ oz/1 cup) raspberries
2 tbsp Honey-Roasted Macadamia Nut Butter (see above)

✿

Honey-roasted macadamia nut butter is swirled through a vanilla-scented nice cream, then spiked with fresh raspberries. Heavenly. Any leftover nut butter keeps beautifully in the fridge for a good couple of weeks. Try it spooned straight from the jar, smothered on toast, or scooped into little Graola Bowls (page 137) as shown!

Preheat the oven to 180°C (350°F/Gas 4). Line a baking sheet with parchment paper.

First make the nut butter. In a bowl, mix the honey, coconut oil, cinnamon and salt. Add the nuts and thoroughly combine. Spread the mixture on to the lined baking sheet in a single layer and bake for 15 minutes or until golden brown. Keep an eye on the nuts to make sure they don't burn.

Remove from the oven and set aside to cool. Once cooled, put the roasted nuts in a food processor or blender and blitz until smooth. Transfer into an airtight container and store in a cool dry place or the fridge. This will last for 3–4 weeks.

To make the nice cream, put the bananas, coconut milk and vanilla extract in a food processor and blend until thick and creamy, scraping down the sides every 30 seconds. The mixture should be the consistency of soft-serve ice cream. Fold through the raspberries and the nut butter – being careful not to over-mix – to make a nice swirl. Serve straight away.

COOKIE DOUGH NICE CREAM

Serves 4

For the raw cookie dough:
3 tbsp melted coconut oil • 100 g (3½ oz/½ cup) coconut sugar
140 g (5 oz/½ cup) crunchy peanut butter
1 tsp vanilla extract • 100 g (3½ oz/¾ cup) buckwheat flour
¼ tsp bicarbonate of soda (baking soda) • a pinch of salt
1–2 tbsp almond milk
30 g (1 oz/¼ cups) dark chocolate chips

For the peanut butter nice cream:
4 bananas, peeled and frozen
400 ml (14 fl oz) tinned coconut milk, chilled (thick part only)
2 tbsp peanut butter • 2 tbsp maple syrup

Cookie dough has to be one of the best things ever, and this version is no exception. No refined sugar and dairy-free, yet you'd never know it from how good it tastes. You can opt to eat it on its own as a lovely little snack, but swirled through peanut butter nice cream takes it to the next level. For ultimate indulgence, I love to serve this in my Edible Chocolate Bowls (page 143).

For the cookie dough, combine the coconut oil, coconut sugar, peanut butter and vanilla extract in a bowl. Add the flour, bicarbonate of soda and salt and stir to form a soft dough that is ever so slightly crumbly. Add the almond milk for a bit of moisture, and stir in the chocolate chips.

To make the nice cream, put the bananas, coconut milk, peanut butter and maple syrup in a food processor and blend until thick and creamy, scraping down the sides every 30 seconds. Process until the mixture becomes completely smooth and the consistency of soft-serve ice cream.

Next, crumble three-quarters of the cookie dough into the nice cream and pour into a freezer-proof container. Scatter the rest of the dough over the top and pop back into the freezer for a couple of hours to firm up, then serve.

PISTACHIO NICE CREAM

❋

Serves 4

150 g (5 oz/1 cup) unsalted pistachios, shelled
155 g (5½ oz/1 cup) cashews, soaked for 4–6 hours • 3 bananas, peeled and frozen
185 ml (6 fl oz) maple syrup or honey • 80 ml (2½ fl oz) coconut oil, melted
2 tsp almond extract • ¼ tsp sea salt

❋

Pistachio ice cream is one of those things that has to be tasted to be believed. Our dairy-free, banana-based version is a thing of wonder. It's ludicrously creamy and will give the classic pistachio gelato a run for its money.

Blitz 100 g (3½ oz/¾ cup) pistachios in a coffee grinder or food processor until you have a fine powder. Set aside. Roughly chop the remaining pistachios.

Drain and rinse the soaked cashews. Put in a high-speed blender or food processor, along with the bananas, ground pistachios, maple syrup, coconut oil, almond extract and salt. Blend on a high speed until completely smooth; this could take a couple of minutes. Add the reserved chopped pistachios to the mix and give it a good stir.

You can pour this into an ice-cream maker and prepare according to the manufacturer's instructions, but it also works beautifully served straight from the blender. Alternatively, pop it into a freezer-proof container and freeze for about 3 hours, stirring every 30 minutes to prevent ice crystals.

ROCKY ROAD NICE CREAM

Serves 2

For the chocolate nice cream:
2 bananas, peeled and frozen • 2 pitted dates
1 tbsp unsweetened cacao powder or cocoa powder

For the vanilla nice cream:
2 bananas, peeled and frozen • 1 tsp vanilla extract

Optional toppings:
cacao chips • chopped dates • The Ultimate Butterscotch Caramel Sauce (page 131)
crushed pecans • crushed pistachios • coconut chunks
dried mulberries • dried cranberries • crumbled almonds
quinoa puffs • pumpkin seeds

You can't go wrong with this recipe. Swirl together the chocolate and vanilla nice cream and then add from the list of toppings. Don't panic if you don't have them all to hand, just try to make sure you have a mix of chewy dates and crunchy nuts, and it will be delicious.

Blend each nice cream separately in a food processor, then place both in a bowl and gently swirl them together with your chosen toppings. Eat straight away.

PINA COLADA NICE CREAM

❋

Serves 1

2 bananas, peeled and frozen • 85 g (3 oz/½ cup) pineapple chunks
125 ml (4 fl oz) tinned coconut milk, chilled (thick part only) • 25 g (1 oz/¼ cup) desiccated coconut

Optional toppings:
fresh pineapple • coconut shavings • pomegranate seeds • banana slices

❋

A taste of the tropics – if you eat this and close your eyes, you can almost feel the sand between your toes. It's both refreshing and delicious.

Put everything in the food processor and blend until thick and creamy, scraping down the sides every 30 seconds. Process until the mixture becomes completely smooth and has the consistency of soft-serve ice cream. Serve in a scooped-out pineapple and top with fresh fruit and a cocktail umbrella for the ultimate retro look.

CLUB TROPICANA

❋

Serves 1

2 bananas, peeled and frozen • ½ ripe papaya, cut into chunks
¼ mango, cut into chunks • zest and juice of ½ lime • seeds and pulp of 1 passion fruit

❋

Get creative with the presentation; think scooped-out pineapples, papayas and coconut halves to go full-throttle on the tropical vibe.

Put all the ingredients, but only half the passion fruit seeds and pulp in the food processor and blend until thick and creamy. Process until the mixture becomes completely smooth and the consistency of soft-serve ice cream. Serve with the remaining passion fruit pulp and seeds on top for a veritable feast!

BREAKFAST

BLACKCURRANT AND COCONUT NICE CREAM WITH CHIA PUDDING AND MANGO

Serves 1

For the chia pudding:
1 tbsp chia seeds • 125 ml (4 fl oz) almond milk
1 tbsp desiccated coconut
1 tsp maple syrup

For the blackcurrant and coconut nice cream:
2 bananas, peeled and frozen
125 ml (4 fl oz) tinned coconut milk, chilled (thick part only)
60 g (2 oz/½ cup) blackcurrants • 1 tsp vanilla extract
1 tbsp agave syrup (optional)

Topping:
½ fresh mango

Chia pudding is a great make-ahead breakfast; the perfect start for mornings when we are rushed off our feet but want something filling and delicious. Prep the pudding the night before, then when ready to serve, top with blackcurrant and coconut nice cream and lots of fresh mango for a beautiful breakfast.

Place all the chia pudding ingredients in a bowl, stir together and pop in the fridge for about 4 hours, or overnight.

Put the ingredients for the nice cream in a food processor and blend until thick and creamy, scraping down the sides every 30 seconds. Process until the mixture becomes completely smooth and has the consistency of soft-serve ice cream.

When ready to eat, layer the blackcurrant and coconut nice cream, chia pudding and mango in a tall glass and serve immediately.

SPIRULINA PROTEIN SOFT-SERVE NICE CREAM

❋

Serves 1

2 bananas, peeled and frozen
½ tsp spirulina powder · 1 scoop vanilla protein powder
½ avocado · 1 Medjool date
½ tsp maca powder (optional)

Optional toppings:
fresh banana slices · strawberries · 1 tbsp bee pollen
chia seeds · grated coconut

❋

Breakfast is the most important meal of the day and adding a healthy dose of protein makes this green-and-bursting-with-goodness nice cream an absolute winner. This is also a fab post-workout snack.

In a food processor or high-speed blender, blend all the ingredients until thick and creamy, scraping down the sides every 30 seconds. Process until the mixture becomes completely smooth and has the consistency of soft-serve ice cream.

Pour into bowl and add your topping(s) of choice.

Top Tip: Turn it into a shake by adding 100–200 ml (3½–7 fl oz) almond milk.

BANOFFEE OVERNIGHT OATS WITH SOFT-SERVE CINNAMON NICE CREAM

❋

Serves 1

For the overnight oats (enough for 4 mornings):
150 g (5 oz/1½ cups) rolled oats · 420 ml (14 fl oz) almond milk
60 ml (2 fl oz) apple juice · 3 tbsp maple syrup · 1 tsp vanilla extract

For the cinnamon nice cream:
2 bananas, peeled and frozen · 1 tsp vanilla extract
½ tsp ground cinnamon · 1 Medjool date · a pinch of salt

Optional toppings:
Caramelised Bananas (page 18) · crumbled pecans
coconut flakes · crumbled cashews
Date Syrup (page 129)

❋

Overnight oats are such a quick and easy breakfast. Make up a big batch at the start of the week, scoop them out daily and serve with toppings of your choice. This recipe is bursting with goodness, and its slow-burn power will keep you going until lunch – a truly delicious start to the day.

To prepare the oats, simply combine all the ingredients in a bowl and then leave to soak overnight in the fridge. The next day, if the mix looks a little dry add more almond milk. Then scoop into a small jar or bowl.

Now, make the cinnamon nice cream. Put the bananas, vanilla extract, cinnamon, date and salt in a food processor and blend until thick and creamy, scraping down the sides every 30 seconds. Process until the mixture becomes completely smooth and has the consistency of soft-serve ice cream.

Scoop the nice cream on top of the oats and add the Caramelised Bananas and any other topping(s) of your choice.

MANGO, BERRY AND LIME NICE-CREAM SLICE

Serves 6

1 handful of fresh raspberries, to fill

For the base:
75 g (2½ oz/¾ cup) rolled oats
4 pitted Medjool dates • 1 tbsp desiccated coconut • ½ tbsp maple syrup
½ tbsp unsweetened cacao powder or cocoa powder (optional)

For the lime nice-cream layer:
1 banana, peeled and frozen • ½ ripe avocado • zest of 3 limes
125 ml (4 fl oz) freshly squeezed lime juice (about 5–6 limes)

For the raspberry nice-cream layer:
1 banana, peeled and frozen • 125 g (4 oz/1 cup) raspberries, fresh or frozen
1 tbsp coconut yoghurt or tinned coconut milk, chilled (thick part only)
2 tbsp almond milk

For the mango nice-cream layer:
1 banana, peeled and frozen
160 g (5 oz/1 cup) mango chunks (about ½ mango)
1 tbsp coconut yoghurt or tinned coconut milk, chilled (thick part only)
2 tbsp almond milk

Toppings:
freeze-dried raspberries • raspberry powder • crushed pistachios

This may not look like your average breakfast but to be honest, there is nothing average about this. Creamy, yet refreshing, bursting with goodness and as pretty as a picture. Obviously you can enjoy this any time of the day, but I do love it for breakfast. Whip this up for a lovely summery morning and enjoy a great start to the day.

continued overleaf

Line the inside of a 21 × 11 × 7 cm (8 × 4 × 3 in) loaf tin with cling film (plastic wrap).

Blend the ingredients for the base together in a food processor, and press into the bottom of the lined loaf tin.

For the lime layer, blend together all the ingredients to form a thick and creamy nice cream. Pour into the prepared tin, on top of the base. Pop in the freezer to firm up for 20 minutes or so, then scatter over the fresh raspberries.

Blend the ingredients for the raspberry nice-cream layer. Spread this over the fresh raspberries in the tin and freeze for another 20 minutes to firm up.

Repeat with the mango layer, blitzing all the ingredients together and then pouring into the tin, on top of the raspberry nice-cream layer.

Once all the layers are assembled, stick 6 lollipop sticks into the loaf at equal intervals and sprinkle the surface with the freeze-dried raspberries, raspberry powder and crushed pistachios.

Leave in the freezer to firm up for a good couple of hours. When ready to serve, slice into portions and enjoy.

COCONUT PORRIDGE WITH CHOCOLATE NICE CREAM AND FRESH BERRIES

Serves 1

For the coconut porridge:
100 g (3½ oz/1 cup) oats (or gluten-free variety) • 150 ml (5 fl oz) coconut water
150 ml (5 fl oz) tinned coconut milk, chilled (thick part only)
75 ml (2½ fl oz) coconut cream

For the chocolate nice cream:
5 bananas, peeled and frozen
500 ml (17 fl oz) tinned coconut milk, at room temperature
250 ml (8½ fl oz) almond milk • 65 g (2 oz/⅔ cup) unsweetened cocoa powder
4 tbsp honey • 1 tsp vanilla extract • 2 heaped tbsp almond butter • ½ tsp xanthan gum

Toppings:
1 handful of fresh or frozen berries

There are few things more lovely than waking up to a creamy bowl of hot coconut porridge. Try adding a cooling dollop of chocolate nice cream and bursts of fresh berries and, trust me, breakfasts will never be the same. This recipe will make enough nice cream for around 4–6 servings, but I'm sure you won't find it a problem to have a little extra.

The night before, soak the oats in the coconut water. The next day, place the coconut milk and cream in a small saucepan, bring to the boil and add the soaked oats. Turn the heat down to a simmer and stir for 3–5 minutes, adding a little more water or coconut milk if it gets too thick. Once cooked, take the pan off the heat and scoop the porridge into a bowl. Cover to keep warm.

For the chocolate nice cream, simply blend all the ingredients together, then pour into a freezer-proof container, cover and freeze, taking out to stir every couple hours to aerate.

To serve, scoop the nice cream straight onto the hot bowl of porridge. (Reheat the porridge if need be.) Scatter with fresh or frozen berries.

NICE CREAM AND GRANOLA

Cool and creamy nice cream with the crunch of granola is a hard combination to beat. These are perfect with the granola recipe on pages 135–136.

RASPBERRY RIPPLE COCONUT NICE CREAM

❋

Serves 4

150 g (5 oz/1¼ cups) raspberries • 2 bananas, peeled and frozen
200 ml (7 fl oz) tinned coconut milk, chilled (thick part only)
85 g (3 oz/¾ cup) cashews, soaked for 4 hours • 60 ml (2 fl oz) maple syrup
1½ tbsp melted coconut oil • ½ tbsp cornflour (cornstarch)
1 tsp vanilla extract • a pinch of sea salt

❋

Blitz three-quarters of the raspberries in a food processor and set aside. Next, blitz the remaining ingredients, except for the leftover raspberries. Stir through the blended raspberries and reserved whole raspberries. Pour into a container, cover and freeze for 2 hours, or until scoopable. Serve in bowls with granola.

MANGO AND PASSION FRUIT NICE CREAM

❋

Serves 4

200 ml (7 fl oz) almond milk • 2 bananas, peeled and frozen • 100 g (3½ oz) mango
pulp of 1 passion fruit • 85 g (3 oz/¾ cup) cashews, soaked for 4 hours
60 ml (2 fl oz) honey • 1½ tbsp light olive oil • ½ tbsp cornflour (cornstarch)
1 tsp vanilla extract • a pinch of sea salt

❋

Blitz all the ingredients in a food processor until thick and creamy. Pour into a container, cover and freeze for 2 hours, or until scoopable. Serve in bowls with granola.

FLOURLESS BANANA PANCAKES WITH CHERRY VANILLA NICE CREAM

❋

Serves 2

For the pancakes (makes 12 small pancakes):
2 bananas (180 g/6½ oz), peeled
7 tbsp milk (I use almond but any milk will be good)
100 g (3 oz/1 cup) rolled oats • 1-2 tbsp coconut oil, for frying

For the cherry vanilla nice cream:
150 g (5 oz/¾ cup) pitted cherries
4 bananas, peeled and frozen • 1 tsp vanilla extract
1 tbsp brown sugar or coconut sugar
¼ tsp ground cinnamon • zest of ½ lemon

❋

These banana pancakes are my favourite thing to make on a lazy weekend morning. If sharing them with other people, you can make the pancakes in advance and warm them gently in the oven whilst you whip-up the cherry soft-serve nice cream.

First, make the pancakes. In a blender or food processor, blitz all the pancake ingredients (except the coconut oil) until nice and smooth. Heat a non-stick frying pan (skillet) over a medium heat and grease with coconut oil. Fry spoonfuls of the batter until you can flip them and then cook for another minute on the other side.

To make the cherry vanilla nice cream, take 100 g (3½ oz/½ cup) of the cherries, chop them in half and set aside. Put the remaining ingredients in a food processor and blend until thick and creamy, scraping down the sides every 30 seconds. Process until the mixture becomes completely smooth and has the consistency of soft-serve ice cream. Then stir in the reserved chopped cherries.

Enjoy the nice cream straight away, scooped on top of the pancakes.

Top Tip: The pancakes can sometimes be a little fiddly to flip, so just spoon over some coconut oil to help the top brown and cook before flipping.

WAFFLES WITH PEACH MELBA NICE CREAM AND RASPBERRY SWIRL

❋

Makes 6 waffles or serves 3–6

For the waffles:
225 g (8 oz/1½ cups) plain (all-purpose) flour
1 tbsp baking powder • 1 tbsp coconut sugar
a pinch of sea salt • 2 large eggs • 310 ml (10½ fl oz) almond milk
60 ml (2 fl oz) coconut oil, melted or vegetable oil
1 tsp vanilla extract

For the peach melba nice cream:
125 g (4 oz/1 cup) tinned peaches, drained, plus extra to serve
250 ml (8½ fl oz) tinned coconut milk, chilled (thick part only) • 2 bananas, peeled and frozen
125 g (4 oz/1 cup) cashews, soaked for 4-6 hours, then drained
60 ml (2 fl oz) coconut oil, melted or vegetable oil • 60 ml (2 fl oz) honey
60 g (2 oz/¼ cup) cane sugar • 1 tsp vanilla extract

For the raspberry swirl:
125 g (4 oz/1 cup) raspberries, fresh or frozen
2 tbsp maple syrup

❋

Peach melba is such a classic combination. You can use either fresh or tinned peaches, although for this recipe, I prefer using tinned as they tend to be more flavourful.

Preheat the waffle iron. Whisk the flour, baking powder, coconut sugar and salt in a bowl. Add the remaining ingredients, whisking until just blended. Let the batter sit for 5 minutes. Ladle enough batter to cover about two-thrids of the surface of the waffle iron and cook until golden.

To make the peach melba nice cream, blend half the peaches with the remaining ingredients. Then stir in the remaining peaches so you get some nice chunks. Set aside.

Make the raspberry swirl, by mashing the raspberries and maple syrup together. Swirl the raspberry mixture through the peach melba nice cream. Allow to set in the freezer for a couple of hours before serving on top of the waffles alongside slices of peach.

Note: Ideally, you'll need a waffle iron for this recipe but you can just treat the waffle batter as pancakes if you don't have the kit.

SMOOTHIES AND SHAKES

SMOOTHIE BOWLS

I absolutely love making smoothie bowls. The flavour combinations are endless, plus there is something inordinately satisfying about eating a smoothie with a spoon...

RASPBERRY, MINT AND COCONUT SMOOTHIE BOWL

Serves 1

1 banana, peeled and frozen • 125 g (4 oz/1 cup) raspberries
125 ml (4 fl oz) tinned coconut milk, chilled (thick part only) • 3–5 fresh mint leaves
1 heaped tsp desiccated coconut

Topping:
sliced strawberries

Blend all the ingredients together in a food processor until thick and creamy, scraping down the sides every 30 seconds. Add more coconut milk or water if it's too thick. Pour into a bowl and top with the sliced strawberries.

PINK SMOOTHIE BOWL

Serves 1

1 banana, peeled and frozen • 90 g (3 oz/½ cup) strawberries
60 g (2 oz/½ cup) raspberries • 1 tbsp almond butter • 125 ml (4 fl oz) almond milk
125 ml (4 fl oz) beetroot juice or 1 tsp beetroot powder (optional)

Topping:
sliced kiwi

Blend everything together in a food processor until thick and creamy, scraping down the sides every 30 seconds. Pour into a bowl and top with slices of kiwi.

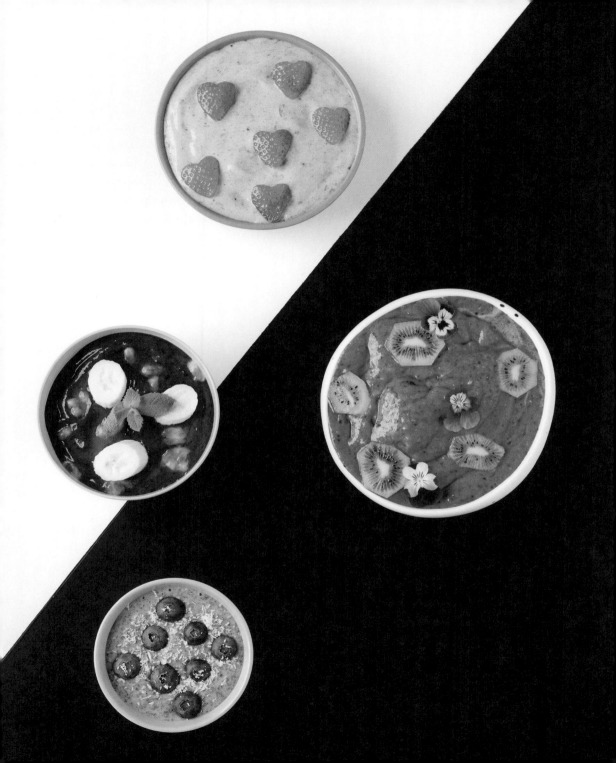

AVOCADO AND BLUEBERRY SMOOTHIE BOWL

Serves 1

1 banana, peeled and frozen • small handful of spinach or kale
125 ml (4 fl oz) apple juice • ½ ripe avocado • a good squeeze of lemon juice
thumb-sized piece of ginger, peeled

Topping:
1 handful of blueberries • grated coconut

Blend everything together in a food processor until thick and creamy, scraping down the sides every 30 seconds. Process until the mixture becomes completely smooth. Pour into a bowl and top with the blueberries and coconut.

BLUEBERRY, COCONUT AND AÇAÍ SMOOTHIE BOWL

Serves 1

½ banana, peeled and frozen • 1 packet (around 100 g/3½ oz) frozen açaí purée
80 g (3 oz/½ cup) frozen blueberries • ½ tbsp agave or maple syrup
125 ml (4 fl oz) pomegranate juice

Toppings:
sliced bananas • pulp of 1 passion fruit

Put the banana, açaí purée, frozen berries, and agave in a blender. Add the pomegranate juice and process until the mixture becomes completely smooth. Pour into a bowl and top with the bananas and passion fruit and enjoy.

CHOCOLATE PROTEIN NANA SMOOTHIE SHAKE

❋

Serves 1

*1 banana, peeled and frozen • 250 ml (8½ fl oz) almond milk
1 tbsp smooth peanut butter • ¼ tsp ground cinnamon
1 scoop chocolate protein powder • 1 tsp maple syrup
1 tsp vanilla extract • ice cubes (optional)*

❋

This is one of my favourite shakes. It's really delicious, filling and full of protein. Perfect for post-workout or for when you are in need of a satisfying something to keep you going.

Put the banana in a food processor and blend until thick and creamy, scraping down the sides every 30 seconds. Process until the mixture becomes completely smooth and has the consistency of soft-serve ice cream. Add the rest of the ingredients to the blender and blitz again, until smooth. For an extra-cold smoothie, add a few ice cubes. If it's too thick, add a little more almond milk.

BANANA SPLIT NICE-CREAM SUNDAE WITH SALTED CARAMEL CHOCOLATE BISCUITS

✳

Serves 1

1 banana, peeled and frozen
2 pitted dates · ½ tsp unsweetened cacao powder or cocoa powder
½ tsp carob powder or cocoa powder · 240-360 ml (8-12½ fl oz) almond milk

Topping:
Whipped Coconut Cream (page 141)
Salted Caramel Chocolate Biscuit (page 89)

✳

All the best parts of a banana split whipped up into a sundae. To top it all off, try this with our magical Salted Caramel Chocolate Biscuits (page 89) for extra indulgence.

Put the bananas, dates, cacao and carob powders in a food processor and blend until thick and creamy, scraping down the sides every 30 seconds. Process until the mixture becomes completely smooth and the consistency of soft-serve ice cream. Add the almond milk and blend again. You want it pouring consistency, so add a little more almond milk or water if needed to loosen it.

To serve, pour into a tall glass and top with a spoon or two of Whipped Coconut Cream. Stick in a straw and serve with a biscuit!

Top Tip: If you forget to freeze your bananas in advance, don't worry! You can cheat by using an ordinary banana and some ice cubes.

GREEN MACHINE
NICE-CREAM SMOOTHIE

❋

Serves 1

1½ bananas, peeled and frozen • ½ ripe avocado
1 big handful of spinach • 40 g (1½ oz/¼ cup) fresh chopped pineapple
100–150 ml (3½–5 fl oz) freshly squeezed orange juice

❋

This spinach, avocado and banana smoothie is unbelievably good. Bursting with goodness, the pineapple provides that natural sweetness, whilst the avocado lends a lovely creamy texture. It's a great green machine to get you going.

Pop the bananas, avocado and spinach into a blender and blitz to make a vibrant green spinach nice cream. Then add the pineapple, and orange juice as needed, and blend to combine. Add a little more water, if necessary, to get the consistency you like.

BLUEBERRY AND
COCONUT SMOOTHIE

❋

Serves 1

1 banana, peeled and frozen • 80 g (3 oz/½ cup) frozen blueberries
125 g (4 oz/½ cup) coconut yoghurt • 2 tbsp desiccated coconut

Bursting with flavour, this is a lovely little smoothie that is both satisfying and good for you.

Put all the ingredients in a food processor and blend until thick, creamy and completely smooth, scraping down the sides every 30 seconds. Pour into a glass and serve immediately.

GREEN GOODNESS
CREAMY CASHEW SMOOTHIE

Serves 1

120 ml (4 fl oz) almond milk • 120 ml (4 fl oz) coconut water
1 banana, peeled and frozen • 40 g (1½ oz/¼ cup) cashews, soaked for 4-6 hours, then drained
25 g (1 oz/¼ cup) mango chunks • 1 big handful of kale

This creamy green concoction is dreamy. Throw in a handful of kale or spinach to add another dose of goodness.

Simply place everything, except the kale into a powerful blender and blend until smooth. Add the kale and blend once more. Pour into a glass and serve cold.

HOT CHOCOLATE

Serves 1

125 ml (4 fl oz) rice milk or milk of choice • 2 tbsp dark chocolate chips
½ tsp cocoa powder • ¼ tsp vanilla extract • a tiny pinch of chilli powder (optional)
a pinch of salt • 1 medium banana, peeled and sliced

Take it to the next level and add a dollop of nice cream (of choice) to your hot chocolate.

Combine the rice milk, chocolate chips, cocoa powder, vanilla extract, chilli powder (if desired) and salt in a small saucepan. Gently heat, stirring constantly. Just as the drink begins to simmer, pour it into a blender, add the banana and blend until smooth and creamy.

MANGO, COCONUT AND TURMERIC LASSI

❋

Serves 1

1 banana, peeled and frozen • 2 tbsp coconut yoghurt
½ mango, peeled and destoned • 375 ml (12½ fl oz) tinned coconut milk, chilled (thick part only)
½ tsp ground cinnamon • ¼–½ tsp ground turmeric
1 tsp coconut oil

Toppings:
Whipped Coconut Cream (page 141)
banana slices
1 handful of raspberries

❋

Here is such a delicious combination of frozen banana and mango with a kick from the powerful spice, turmeric. Turmeric makes an unusual but delightfully surprising smoothie.

Simply blend everything together in a blender or food processor until smooth. Pour into a glass, layered with the Whipped Coconut Cream and serve topped with the bananas and raspberries.

POPS AND LOLLIES

FROZEN BANANA POPS

❋

Makes 10

10 ripe bananas
200 g (7 oz) dark chocolate (minimum 70% cocoa), coarsely chopped
4 tbsp coconut oil

Optional toppings:
sea salt · goji berries · toasted flaked almonds, roughly chopped
lightly toasted buckwheat groats · freeze-dried raspberries
toasted unsweetened coconut flakes or desiccated coconut · chopped pistachios
grated chocolate · cacao nibs · crushed rose petals · chopped peanuts
puffed brown rice · melted almond butter

❋

This is the ultimate frozen banana treat. They are really fun and simple to make, they taste amazing and you can dress them up in so many different ways. These pops are perfect for children's parties but also go down exceptionally well with grown-ups. You can make them ahead and bring them out as a delicious treat. It's also quite fun to just prepare the frozen banana pops first, then lay out the melted chocolate and all the toppings so everyone can dip their own!

Line a baking sheet with parchment paper. Peel the bananas, halve horizontally and insert a wooden skewer, lollipop stick or cake pop stick into the cut side of each piece of banana. If you have giant bananas you can always cut them down a little and save the excess for some nice cream. Place the prepared bananas on the lined baking sheet and put in the freezer for at least 1 hour, or ideally overnight.

Melt the chocolate and coconut oil in a heatproof bowl suspended over a pan that's half-full of simmering water. Stir together until smooth. Dip each frozen banana piece in the chocolate, twirling to coat. You may find this easiest if you first pour the chocolate into a tall glass. Then roll, sprinkle or douse in your chosen toppings.

Place back on the lined tray and return to the freezer until ready to serve. Allow to thaw slightly before eating. If not serving within 24 hours, store in an airtight container or freezer bag for up to a week, making sure you put parchment paper between the pops to ensure they don't stick together.

DOUBLE CHOCOLATE SALTED CARAMEL NICE-CREAM LOLLIES

❋

Makes 6

For the nice cream:
2 bananas, peeled and frozen • 500 ml (17 fl oz) coconut milk, chilled (thick part only)
1 vanilla pod, seeds scraped or 1 tsp vanilla extract • 1 tsp maple syrup

For the salted caramel:
120 g (4 oz/½ cup) almond butter • 125 ml (4 fl oz) coconut oil, melted
120 ml (4 fl oz) maple syrup • 2 tsp vanilla extract
a pinch or 2 of sea salt

For the chocolate shell:
300 g (10½ oz) dark chocolate (minimum 70% cocoa)
80 ml (3 fl oz) coconut oil, melted

❋

Incredibly indulgent and creamy, with a layer of salted caramel, these lollies are encased in rich dark chocolate. Whip up a big batch of these and serve them for pudding after a dinner party – people absolutely love them. Mind you, that's only if you can bear to share them...

For the nice cream, blend the ingredients together until smooth and creamy. Pour the mixture into your popsicle moulds, add a popsicle stick into each and place in the freezer for 3-4 hours or overnight, to set.

Make the caramel by blending all the ingredients in a food processor until smooth and creamy.

For the chocolate shell, melt the ingredients in a heatproof bowl suspended over a pan that's half-full of simmering water until well combined. Leave to cool.

Line a baking tray with parchment paper. Take the pops out of the freezer and run the moulds under warm water. Don't use hot water or the pops will melt and won't hold their shape! Firmly pull up on the sticks and carefully remove the pops from the mould. Dip the pops in the chocolate, then arrange on the tray. The chocolate should harden straight away. Spread the caramel evenly over each pop then put them back on the tray and freeze for 10 minutes. Once hardened, dip them in the chocolate again. Freeze for 30 minutes to set. Sprinkle with sea salt before serving.

TRIPLE CHOCO-TASTIC NICE-CREAM POPSICLES WITH TOASTED ALMOND CHOCOLATE SHELL

✳

Makes 6

For the chocolate nice cream:
250 ml (8½ fl oz) tinned coconut milk, chilled (thick part only)
2 large bananas, peeled and frozen • ½ tbsp unsweetened cacao powder or cocoa powder
2 tbsp maple syrup (optional) • 6 squares of dark chocolate

For the toasted almond chocolate shell:
250 g (9 oz/2 cups) whole almonds • 340 g (12 oz/2 cups) dark chocolate chips
100 g (4 oz/½ cup) coconut oil

✳

These are the ultimate chocolate nice cream popsicles. The hard chocolate centre and crunchy nut coating take them to the next level. A must for chocolate lovers.

Make the nice cream by blitzing all the ingredients (except the chocolate squares) in a blender until smooth. Tip the mixture into the popsicle moulds and place a block of chocolate into the middle of each one. Slide in the popsicle sticks and freeze for 3 hours or overnight.

For the toasted almond chocolate shell first preheat the oven to 180°C (350°F/Gas 4). Scatter the almonds on a baking sheet, place in the oven and toast until golden. Remove and allow to cool, then chop the almonds into small pieces. Melt the chocolate and coconut oil in a heatproof bowl suspended over a pan of simmering water. Stir until smooth. Set aside to cool slightly, then mix in the chopped, toasted almonds.

Line a baking sheet with parchment paper. When the pops are fully frozen, run the moulds under warm water. Don't use hot water or the pops will melt and won't hold their shape! Firmly pull up on the sticks and carefully remove the pops from the mould. Dip the pops into the chocolate nut mix and arrange them in a single layer on the prepared tray.

Freeze for at least 30 minutes to allow the chocolate to harden. To store, put each frozen pop between pieces of parchment paper and freeze for up to 3 weeks.

Top Tip: Yoghurt pots work really well here if you don't have proper popsicle moulds.

ORANGE BANANA SMOOTHIE POPS

✿

Makes 6

250 g (8 oz/1 cup) coconut yoghurt
170 ml (5½ fl oz) freshly squeezed orange juice, plus zest of 1 orange
2 large bananas, peeled and frozen
zest of 1 lime • 1 tbsp freshly squeezed lime juice

✿

These are perfect on a summery day. Everyone loves them, and they are always a hit with everyone, particularly the kids

Purée the coconut yoghurt, orange juice, orange zest, bananas, lime zest and fresh lime juice in a blender or food processor. Pour into 6 moulds, add a stick to each mould. Freeze until the smoothie pops are solid (about 4 hours).

To release the pops, dip the moulds into warm water. Don't use hot water or the pops will melt and won't hold their shape! Firmly pull up on the sticks and carefully remove the pops from the mould.

Top Tip: Paper cups work really well for these pops – just lightly grease the cups with coconut oil to ensure they don't stick. There is something very satisfying about peeling off the paper cup to release the lolly!

MATCHA AND BLACKBERRY COCONUT BREAKFAST POPS

❋

Makes 8 small pops

65 g (2½ oz/½ cup) fresh blackberries
60 ml (2 fl oz) maple syrup
130 g (4½ oz/½ cup) coconut yoghurt · 1 tbsp melted coconut oil
2 bananas, peeled and frozen · ½ tsp vanilla extract
1 tbsp matcha powder

❋

This is such a dreamy flavour combination. Trust me when I tell you that amongst other things, these make an ideal breakfast – especially when you have a million things to do and are rushing out the door.

Rinse and purée the blackberries in a food processor or mash with a potato masher. Push the berries through a fine mesh sieve to get rid of the seeds. Combine the berries with the maple syrup, 2 tablespoons of coconut yoghurt and the melted coconut oil. Set aside.

In a food processor or blender, blitz 1 banana and the vanilla extract until smooth and creamy, scraping down the sides every 30 seconds. Set aside.

Blend the remaining banana with the matcha and the rest of the coconut yoghurt, until the mixture is creamy and pale green in colour.

Carefully drop a spoonful of the matcha nice cream into the bottom of each popsicle mould. Follow with a spoonful of the blackberry purée and then the vanilla nice cream. Repeat until the pop-moulds are full but not overflowing.

Insert the popsicle sticks into mould, leaving about 3.5 cm (1½ in) exposed. Pop into the freezer for at least a few hours.

To release pops, dip the moulds into warm water. Don't use hot water or the pops will melt and won't hold their shape! Firmly pull up on the sticks and carefully remove the pops from the mould. If you want to save the pops for later, simply lay them flat on a baking sheet lined with parchment paper. Once they have frozen solid you can store them in a Ziploc® freezer bag.

ROSE, PISTACHIO AND RASPBERRY NICE-CREAM LOLLIES

❁

Makes 4–6 lollies

4 bananas, peeled and frozen
4 tbsp Pistachio Nut Butter (opposite page)
1 tbsp rose water • 2-3 tbsp agave syrup
60 ml (2 fl oz) cacao butter, melted or melted coconut or olive oil
1 handful of fresh or frozen raspberries

Toppings:
Pistachio Nut Butter, melted
1 handful of pistachios, chopped
1 handful of rose petals
1 handful of free-dried raspberries

❁

Such a beautiful flavour combination and so refreshing – these lollies are simply wonderful.

Put the bananas in a food processor and blend until thick and creamy, scraping down the sides every 30 seconds. Process until the mixture becomes smooth and creamy.

Next add the Pistachio Nut Butter, rose water, agave, melted cacao butter and blend. Stir in the raspberries and then pour the mixture into the moulds. Add the sticks and then place them into the freezer. Freeze for 2-3 hours until set solid.

Once frozen, run the moulds under warm water. Don't use hot water or the pops will melt and won't hold their shape! Firmly pull up on the sticks and carefully remove the pops from the mould.

To serve, drizzle with melted Pistachio Nut Butter and sprinkle with chopped pistachios, rose petals and freeze-dried raspberries.

PISTACHIO NUT BUTTER

❋

Makes 1 × 300 g jar (10½ oz/1⅓ cups)

2 cups unsalted shelled pistachio
¼ tsp salt · 1 tbsp honey

❋

Nut butters are so easy to make and are delicious when blitzed up in a nice cream. If you don't like pistachios feel free to use any nut of choice!

Preheat the oven to 180°C (350°F/Gas 4). Spread the pistachios on a baking sheet and bake in the oven for 5 minutes or until just fragrant and starting to brown.

Tip the pistachios into the food processor and blend for about 10 minutes until thick and creamy. Add the salt and honey, then stir to combine.

Store in a sealed container in the fridge for several weeks.

CHERRY POPS WITH DOUBLE CHOCOLATE AND VANILLA MAGIC SHELL

Makes about 6

For the cherry nice cream:
5 bananas, peeled and frozen • 125 ml (4 fl oz) coconut milk, chilled (thick part only)
1 × 380 g (13½ oz) jarred black cherries

For the dark chocolate shell:
340 g (12 oz/2 cups) dark chocolate chips
100 g (3½ oz/½ cups) coconut oil

For the white chocolate vanilla magic shell:
200 g (7 oz/1½ cups) white chocolate chips • 2 tbsp coconut oil
1 vanilla bean, seeds scraped, or 2 tsp vanilla extract

Topping:
freeze-dried raspberries

I love the use of two types of chocolate here. It works so well with the cherry nice cream, which makes a beautiful lolly on its own if you want a slightly more refreshing treat.

For the cherry nice cream, put the bananas and coconut milk into a food processor and blend until smooth, scraping down the sides every 30 seconds. Add the cherries and blend again to combine. Pour into popsicle moulds, pop a stick in the middle of each and put into the freezer for 2–3 hours to set.

To make the dark chocolate shell, melt the chocolate and coconut oil in a heatproof bowl over a pan of simmering water. Stir the chocolate until smooth and set aside. Make the white chocolate shell in the same way, adding in the vanilla and heating only until just melted. Allow to cool.

Once the pops are frozen, line a tray with parchment paper. Run the moulds under warm water. Don't use hot water or the pops will melt and won't hold their shape! Firmly pull up on the sticks and carefully remove the pops from the mould. Dip each pop in the melted dark chocolate (it will set straight away). Spoon over the melted white chocolate and sprinkle with freeze-dried raspberries. Place the pops on the lined tray and freeze for 30 minutes to firm up. To store, place each pop between pieces of parchment paper and freeze for up to 3 weeks.

PRETTY IN PINK POPSICLES
WITH EDIBLE FLOWERS

❋

Makes about 6

125 g (4 oz/1 cup) raspberries
2 bananas, peeled and frozen
250 ml (8½ fl oz) almond milk
finely grated zest and juice of 1 lime
6 edible flowers or thinly sliced slivers of lime

❋

These little pink beauties are gorgeous inside and out. I love how pretty they are and they just burst with flavour. Raspberries and lime are a match made in heaven.

Simply blend the raspberries, bananas, almond milk and lime zest and juice together in a food processor or blender, until deliciously creamy.

Lay the flowers or lime slices face down in your moulds and spoon in the nice cream. Give the mould a sharp tap on the countertop to release any air bubbles. Insert a popsicle stick and freeze for at least 6 hours. To remove the smoothie pops from their moulds, run the moulds under warm water. Don't use hot water or the pops will melt and won't hold their shape! Firmly pull up on the sticks and carefully remove the pops from the mould and enjoy!

To store, put each frozen pop between pieces of parchment paper and freeze for up to 3 weeks.

Top Tip: Silicone moulds work well for these. Simply place them under running water to make sure they are a little damp and it will help the pops come out easily.

DARK CHOCOLATE PEANUT BUTTER BANANA BITES

❋

Makes about 25 bites

5 large bananas, sliced into 1 cm (½ in) thick rounds
3 tbsp smooth peanut butter or other nut butter
220 g (8 oz) dark chocolate (minimum 62% cocoa), chopped

Toppings:
sea salt flakes, to taste · chopped peanuts

❋

I tend to feel a bit panicky if I don't have a stash of these in the freezer at all times. They are such a perfect snack, for when you need a little something sweet. They are particularly good brought out at a dinner party instead of your standard box of chocolates.

Line 2 baking sheets with parchment paper. Place the banana slices on the lined baking sheets, in a single layer, in rows. Use a spoon to scoop the peanut butter onto half of the banana slices. If you want to be a bit neater, you can transfer the peanut butter to a Ziploc® bag, snip a corner off and pipe the peanut butter on top. Put the remaining, uncoated banana slices on top of the peanut butter ones.

Carefully insert wooden sticks to secure it all together (the peanut butter will want to escape). Pop into the freezer to firm up for about 30 minutes.

Melt the dark chocolate in a heatproof bowl suspended over a pan of simmering water. Stir the chocolate until smooth.

When the pops are frozen, simply dunk in the melted chocolate and sprinkle with sea salt and chopped peanuts. Continue until all the bananas bites have been coated. Pop back on the baking sheets and freeze for 2 hours to harden.

These keep beautifully in the freezer for a good month or so. Just store them in a Ziploc® bag once they are completely hard and eat at your leisure. Before serving, allow the bites to thaw for about 5–10 minutes so that you can bite into them.

Top Tip: Follow the method above but leave out the peanut butter. Dunk the frozen banana slices in chocolate and then add toppings to your heart's delight.

▼▼▼▼▼▼▼▼▼▼▼▼▼▼▼▼

COOKIES AND CAKES

▲▲▲▲▲▲▲▲▲▲▲▲▲▲▲▲

BANANA CHOCOLATE CHIP CHAI NICE-CREAM SANDWICHES WITH GINGER BISCUITS

✻

Makes 5 sandwiches

For the gingerbread cookies:
100 g (3½ oz/½ cup) coconut sugar
2½ tbsp almond butter • 3 tbsp maple syrup • 1 large egg
50 g (2 oz/¼ cup) coconut oil, softened but not melted
1 tbsp ground ginger • ½ tsp ground cinnamon • ¼ tsp ground nutmeg
¼ tsp salt • ½ tsp bicarbonate of soda (baking soda)
130 g (4½ oz/1 cup) buckwheat flour, plus extra to sprinkle
50 g (2 oz/½ cup) oats (or gluten-free)

For the chai nice cream:
60 ml (2 fl oz) almond milk • 100 g (3½ oz/¾ cup) cacao butter
3 chai tea bags (or black tea for a more subtle flavour)
6 large bananas, peeled and frozen
60 g (2 oz/½ cup) cashews, soaked for 4–6 hours, then drained
1 tsp vanilla extract • ½ tsp ground cinnamon • ½ tsp ginger powder
¼ tsp ground cloves • ¼ tsp ground cardamom
a large pinch of Himalayan crystal salt or sea salt
170 g (6 oz/1 cup) dark chocolate chips

✻

Ice-cream sandwiches are so good! You forget how good they are until you have one. The flavour combination of the chai and ginger is really gorgeous. They also have the added bonus of looking a lot more difficult to make than they actually are.

Preheat the oven to 175°C (350°F/Gas 4) and line a baking sheet with parchment paper. To make the cookies, pop the coconut sugar, almond butter, maple syrup, egg, coconut oil, spices, salt and bicarbonate of soda in a bowl, and give it a good whisk. Add the buckwheat flour and oats, then stir until well combined. Your dough should hold its shape when pressed, but not feel dry.

Sprinkle the prepared baking sheet with flour. Generously dust the dough with flour and carefully roll out to a little thicker than 3 mm (⅛ in) on top.

continued overleaf

Use a 7.5 cm (3 in) round cookie cutter to cut out cookie shapes and carefully transfer to the lined baking sheet, leaving about 5 cm (2 in) between them. You may need to dust your cutter in some flour if the dough proves too sticky. Then transfer to the baking sheet and bake for 8–10 minutes, until only slightly browned on the edges as they'll continue to harden as they cool.

Remove from the oven and let the cookies cool completely. (Or for a melty, delicious treat, you can sandwich the warm cookies with the nice cream. Bib optional, but recommended.)

To make the chai nice cream, warm the almond milk and cacao butter in a saucepan until just boiling. Turn off the heat, then add the chai teabags and leave to infuse for 10 minutes. Remove the teabags and discard.

Place the bananas and soaked cashews in a food processor and blend until almost the texture of ice cream. Add the vanilla extract, chai almond milk, cinnamon, ginger, cloves, cardamon and salt and process again for 20 seconds, until you reach the desired consistency.

To assemble the sandwiches, use an ice-cream scoop to scoop out 5 large balls of ice cream and put on the bases of 5 cookies (face down) and then top with another cookie (face up). Use both hands to carefully press the cookies together, applying as much pressure as you dare to sandwich them together. Decorate the nice-cream layer with the chocolate chips (as pictured on the previous page).

Devour straight away, or pop back in the freezer on a lined tray to set. The sandwiches will be happy sitting in the freezer, stored in a Ziploc® bag or freezerproof container, for a good few weeks, though they are best if eaten within the first several days. Before serving, let them thaw slightly for 15 minutes, or if you are impatient like me, give them a zap in the microwave for about 20 seconds.

Top Tip: If the dough is too delicate to handle, pop them in the freezer for 5 minutes to firm up before baking.

CHOCOLATE COFFEE NICE-CREAM SANDWICHES

❉

Makes 10 cookies (5 sandwiches)

For the cookies:
*120 ml (4 fl oz) brown rice milk or any nut milk · 1 tsp lemon juice
65 g (2 oz/⅓ cup) soft brown sugar or coconut sugar · 3 tbsp melted coconut oil
1 tsp vanilla extract · 1 large egg · 120 g (4 oz/1 cup) buckwheat flour
30 g (1 oz/¼ cup) unsweetened cocoa powder
1 tsp bicarbonate of soda (baking soda) · a pinch of sea salt*

For the coffee nice cream:
*6 bananas, peeled and frozen · 3 tbsp peanut butter
2 tbsp coffee liqueur · 60 ml (2 fl oz) almond milk
2 tbsp espresso, chilled · 1 tbsp instant coffee granules · ¼ tsp salt
2 tbsp agave syrup · 2 tbsp brown rice syrup · 2 tbsp melted coconut oil
2 tbsp tinned coconut milk, chilled (thick part only) · 30 g (1 oz/¼ cup) chopped chocolate*

❉

These chocolate cookies are really light and airy, more like little fluffy cakes in the shape of a cookie. They make the perfect exterior for some indulgently delicious nice-cream sandwiches. Swoon.

Preheat the oven to 170°C (340°F/Gas 3), and line a baking tray with parchment paper.

To make the cookies, pour the nut milk and lemon juice in a jug and let it sit for a few minutes (this helps the milk thicken a little). Crack the egg in a bowl, add the coconut sugar, melted coconut oil and vanilla extract, then beat. Add the thickened almond milk and beat again. Stir in the remaining ingredients, beating until well combined.

Spoon 10 tablespoons of the cookie batter onto the prepared baking sheet, leaving a small space between each one. Bake for 7 minutes or until cooked. Remove from the oven, let cool on the sheet for 5 minutes, then carefully transfer to a wire rack to cool completely.

In the meantime, make the coffee nice cream. Put the bananas in a food processor and blend until thick and creamy, scraping down the sides every 30 seconds.

continued overleaf

Process until the mixture becomes completely smooth and the consistency of soft-serve ice cream. Add in the remaining ingredients, except the chopped chocolate, and blend until incorporated. Mix in the chocolate by hand.

Use an ice-cream scoop to scoop out 5 large balls of nice cream and put on the base of 5 cookies (face down) and then top with another cookie (face up).

Use both hands to carefully press the cookies together enclosing the nice cream. Place the sandwiches in a freezer-proof dish, cover with cling film (plastic wrap), and pop back in the freezer. These will stay fresh for up to a week.

Before eating, either let your sandwich sit out of the freezer for about 15 minutes or unwrap it and microwave for 20 seconds. The more frozen the cookie sandwich, the duller the flavour, and the harder your teeth need to be.

SALTED CARAMEL CHOCOLATE BISCUITS

Makes 16 cookies

225 g (8 oz/1¾ cups) buckwheat flour, plus extra to dust
100 g (3½ oz/1 cup) ground almonds (almond meal) • a tiny pinch of sea salt
½ tsp baking powder • 4 tbsp maple syrup • 2 tbsp almond butter
2 tbsp melted coconut oil • 1 tbsp almond milk • 2 large eggs • 10 pitted Medjool dates
2 tbsp almond butter • tiny pinch of sea salt
200 g (7 oz) dark chocolate (minimum 70% cocoa), melted

To make the recipe vegan you can substitute the eggs with flax 'egg', an excellent vegan alternative. Just mix 2 tablespoons flaxseeds and 6 tablespoons water in a bowl and let sit for 5 minutes.

Preheat the oven to 180°C (350°F/Gas 4). Line a baking sheet with parchment paper.

Put the buckwheat flour, ground almonds, salt and baking powder in a bowl and stir. Add the maple syrup, almond butter, coconut oil, almond milk and eggs, giving it all a good stir – you may want to use your hands. It will be a sticky dough.

Dust a work surface with a little buckwheat flour and then tip the dough out. Gently, using your hands or a rolling pin, smooth the dough out until it is 3–4 mm (⅛ in) thick. You can add more flour if it's still too sticky, but don't be too liberal or you will end up with a tough cookie.

Use a round 7 cm (3 in) cookie cutter to cut out the dough and use a palette knife to carefully pop onto the prepared tray. Bake for about 10 minutes, until lovely and golden. Leave to cool completely on a wire rack.

Meanwhile, for the caramel layer, simply blend the dates, almond butter, 1 tablespoon of water and sea salt together in a food processor, until smooth-ish and creamy.

Once the biscuits are cooled, spread them with a layer of caramel. These then need to set in the fridge for 30 minutes. Then either dip the biscuits in the melted chocolate, or spoon the chocolate over and then leave to set. They will keep in an airtight container for up to 5 days.

CHOCOLATE AVOCADO NICE-CREAM FLOWERPOT CAKES

✿

Serves 6

For the black bean brownies:
225 g (8 oz/1½ cups) dark chocolate, broken into chunks.
1 × 400g (14 oz) tin of cooked black beans, rinsed and drained
30 g (1 oz/¼ cup) unsweetened cocoa powder, or cacao powder • 2 large eggs
80 ml (2½ fl oz) coconut oil, melted • ¼ tsp of ground cinnamon
2 tsp vanilla extract • a generous pinch of salt • ½ tsp baking powder
1 tsp instant coffee granules • 2 tsp of maple syrup

For the chocolate avocado nice cream:
4 bananas, peeled and frozen • 2 tsp almond milk, chilled (thick part only) • 1 large ripe avocado
2 tbsp maple syrup • 2 tbsp brown rice syrup or liquid sweetener of choice
4 tbsp unsweetened cacao powder or cocoa powder
1 tsp vanilla extract • ½ tsp sea salt

For the Oreo 'soil':
1 × 154 g (5 ½ oz) packet Oreos

For the flowerpots:
6 × small clay flower pots (300 ml/10 fl oz), or freezer-safe pots, washed and dried
6 × plastic drinking straws • freshly cut flowers of choice

✿

I love bringing these to the table as though they are simply the table decorations and then seeing the surprise on people's faces when you hand them a spoon after dinner and tell them to dig in. This timing actually works really well, as the nice cream pots need time to thaw.

Preheat your oven to 180°C (350°F/Gas 4) and line a 20 × 20 cm (8 × 8 in) baking sheet with baking parchment.

To make the brownies, pop everything into a food processor and blend until it's smooth and creamy. Tip onto your prepared baking tray and smooth the mixture out. Bake in the oven for about 35 minutes, until it's firm to the touch and a toothpick comes out clean-ish. Leave to cool.

continue overleaf

Find a cookie cutter or glass that is roughly the same width as the bottom of your flowerpots, then stamp out 6 circles of brownie. Drop the brownie circles into each of your flowerpots, lightly pressing to make sure they are all the way down.

Hold a straw up against the side of a flowerpot and snip it so it's 1–2.5 cm (½–1 in) shorter than the top rim of the pot. Repeat with the other straws. Stick each straw into the centre of each pot through the brownie.

To make the Oreo 'soil' for the pots, simply blitz up the Oreos in a food processor until they are a fine 'soil' texture.

For the chocolate avocado nice cream, blend together all the ingredients until smooth and creamy like soft-serve ice cream.

To assemble, spoon the chocolate avocado nice cream into the pots on top of the brownie. Work the nice cream around the straw, until it almost reaches the top of the straw. Top with a generous mound of the Oreo 'soil'. Pop a fresh flower into each straw and serve.

If you want to make these ahead, just don't adorn with the flowers. You can keep these in the freezer until you are ready to serve them and then pop the flowers in when you take them out of the freezer. Make sure you allow the pots to soften for 20–25 minutes before serving.

CHOCOLATE, BANANA AND MOCHA WAFFLE CAKE

❋

Serves 4

For the waffles:
2 bananas, mashed • 500 ml (17 fl oz) almond milk
2 tsp vanilla extract • 300 g (10½ oz/2½ cups) plain (all-purpose) flour or gluten-free flour
2 tsp baking powder • 2 tbsp coconut sugar (or honey, agave syrup or brown sugar)
a pinch of sea salt • 3 tbsp unsweetened cacao powder or cocoa powder

For the caramelised bananas:
2 tsp coconut oil • 1 heaped tsp coconut sugar • a tiny pinch of rock salt • 6 fresh bananas, sliced

For the mocha coconut nice cream:
5 bananas, peeled and frozen • 250 ml (8½ fl oz) coconut cream
1 tbsp instant coffee granules • 60 ml (2 fl oz) coconut oil, melted
2 tbsp coffee liquor • 2 tbsp brown rice syrup (optional)

Toppings:
The Ultimate Butterscotch Caramel Sauce (page 131), to serve
Caramel Popcorn (page 139), to serve

❋

These are great waffles in their own right, but try going the whole way and making the waffle nice cream cake for a special occasion. I guarantee it will blow everyone's socks off.

Heat the waffle iron. To make the waffles combine all the ingredients together and mix well, adding a little more milk if necessary (the batter should be thick enough to easily drop off the spoon). Cook the waffles and set aside.

For the caramelised bananas, melt the coconut oil in a pan over a medium heat then add the coconut sugar and salt. Toss in the bananas and coat. Cook until they are golden and gorgeous.

To make the nice cream, simply blend the ingredients in a food processor or blender, until thick and like creamy soft-serve ice cream.

To assemble, layer up the waffles, bananas and coconut nice cream. Drizzle over the Ultimate Butterscotch Sauce and top with the Caramel Popcorn.

DEEP-DISH CHOCOLATE CHIP COOKIE WITH CINNAMON NICE CREAM

Serves 4–6 people

For the cinnamon nice cream:
60 g (2 oz) coconut oil, melted • 2 tsp ground cinnamon
1 tsp vanilla extract • 6 bananas, peeled and frozen • 2 tbsp coconut yoghurt
8 pitted Medjool or ordinary dates, roughly chopped

For the chocolate chip cookie:
2 × 400 g (14 oz) tinned chickpeas (garbanzo beans), drained and rinsed
100 g (3½ oz/1 cup) rolled oats • 90 g (3 oz/⅓ cup) unsweetened apple purée
2 tbsp melted coconut oil • 2 tsp vanilla extract • ½ tsp bicarbonate of soda (baking soda)
2 tsp baking powder • ½ tsp sea salt • 120 ml (4 fl oz) maple syrup
100 g (3½ oz/½ cup) coconut sugar • 160 g (5½ oz/1 cup) dark chocolate chips

Don't shudder when you see beans listed as an ingredient in this cookie recipe. I promise you can't taste them, and they make the most decadent-tasting cookie that is naturally gluten-free and deliciously squidgy. Just don't tell your friends what is in the cookie before they eat it!

For the cinnamon nice cream, simply blend everything together (except the dates) in a food processor until smooth and creamy. Finally, stir in the chopped dates and pop into the freezer to firm up for a couple of hours.

To make the cookie, preheat the oven to 190°C (375°F/Gas 5). Take a round 25 cm (10 in) pie dish and grease it lightly with coconut oil. Put all the ingredients (except the chocolate chips) in a food processor and blend until smooth, scraping down sides every 30 seconds. Fold in the chocolate chips. Pour the mixture into the prepared tin, sprinkle with more chocolate chips if you want, and bake for 35–40 minutes or until firm to the touch. Don't be tempted to over-bake the cookie. Remove from the oven and leave to cool for 10 minutes.

To serve, top with scoops of the cinnamon nice cream and take to the table with lots of spoons so people can dig in. Of course for a more formal affair, slice the cookie up and put on individual plates along with a scoop of nice cream.

MINT CHOCOLATE CHIP NICE-CREAM
WAFFLE SANDWICHES

❋

Makes 5 small waffle sandwiches

For the mint choc chip nice cream:
80 g (3 oz) baby leaf spinach • 4 bananas, peeled and frozen
130 g (5 oz/½ cup) coconut yoghurt • 60 ml (2 fl oz) coconut oil, melted
10 g (¼ oz/½ cup) mint leaves • 1 tbsp peppermint extract • 1 small avocado
60 g (2 oz/½ cup) dark chocolate chips, roughly chopped

For the waffles:
1 large egg • 150 g (5½ oz/1 cup) self raising flour
240 ml (8½ fl oz) almond milk
a pinch of sea salt

❋

Mint choc chip with a healthy dose of... spinach? Salad dodgers, don't panic; it just adds some goodness and a vibrant green. You can't taste it, I promise. I recommend serving these guys for afternoon tea, although a nice cream waffle sandwich for breakfast is pretty hard to beat.

For the nice cream, place the spinach in a blender or food processor with a few tablespoons of water and bitz until smooth. Set aside. Blend the remaining ingredients (except for the chocolate chips) with 1 tablespoon of the spinach purée, until thick and creamy. Stir through the chocolate chips and pop into a freezer-proof container and freeze for 1 hour, until firm.

To make your waffles, first heat your waffle iron. Crack the egg into a large mixing bowl then add the flour, milk and sea salt and whisk everything together until you have a lovely, smooth batter. Pour a couple of tablespoons of the batter at a time into the middle of the waffle maker to make a small round-shaped waffle and cook until puffed and golden.

To serve, scoop the mint choc chip nice cream between two waffles and enjoy.

Note: Ideally, you'll need a waffle iron for this recipe but you can also treat the waffle batter as pancakes if you don't have the kit.

NEAPOLITAN NICE-CREAM CAKE WITH BROWNIES

❋

Serves 10

For the black bean brownies:
(same as brownie recipe on page 91)

For the strawberry nice cream:
80 g (3 oz/½ cup) cashews • 120 ml (4 fl oz) almond milk
2 bananas, peeled and frozen • 150 g (5 oz/1 cup) strawberries, hulled and chopped
juice of ½ lemon • 1 tbsp maple syrup • 125 ml (4 fl oz) coconut oil, melted

For the vanilla nice cream:
80 g (3 oz/½ cup) cashews • 3 bananas, peeled and frozen • 120 ml (4 fl oz) almond milk
60 ml (2 fl oz) coconut oil, melted • 1½ tsp vanilla extract
2 tbsp maple syrup

❋

This is a cake you can bring out for any occasion, even when there isn't an occasion. I love it topped with a tumbling tower of extra brownies and a big gaudy candle or sparkler plonked on for good measure.

Preheat the oven to 180°C (350°F/Gas 4). Take an 18 cm (7 in) round cake tin and line the base with parchment paper. Make the brownie mixture according to the instructions on page 91. Tip the mixture into the prepared tin, smoothing out the surface. Pop into the oven for about 35 minutes, until firm to the touch. Remove from the oven and cool in the tin for 10 minutes then place on to a wire rack to cool completely. Once cool, place back in the tin.

To make the stawberry nice cream, put the cashews in a blender or food processor and pulse to a fine powder, then add the almond milk and blend again. Add the remaining ingredients and blend until thick and creamy. Repeat this same process for the vanilla nice cream. You will have two delightfully creamy nice creams; one pink and the other white.

Scoop the vanilla nice cream over the top of the brownie. Cover with cling film (plastic wrap) and pop into the freezer for 20 minutes to firm up. Spread the strawberry layer on top, then re-cover and return to the freezer for at least 2 hours before serving. Once firm, carefully remove the cake from the tin and leave it to sit at room temperature for 20 minutes. You can always make extra brownies and serve the cake adorned with a pile of extra brownies for an added wow factor.

RAW CHOCOLATE BROWNIE AND AVOCADO NICE-CREAM SANDWICH

❋

Serves 10

For the raw brownie:
150 g (5 oz/1¼ cups) pecans
100 g (3½ oz/½ cup) pitted Medjool dates (or ordinary dates soaked in warm water)
50 g (2 oz/½ cup) unsweetened cacao powder or cocoa powder
50 g (2 oz) coconut oil • 1 tbsp maple syrup, to taste

For the avocado nice cream:
5 large banana, peeled and frozen • 2 medium sized ripe avocados
¼ lemon, juiced • 1 tsp vanilla extract
pinch of salt • 2 tbsp honey

For the chocolate shell:
55 g (2 oz/¼ cup) coconut oil, melted
1-2 tbsp maple syrup or honey • 2 tbsp unsweetened cacao powder or cocoa powder
a pinch of sea salt

❋

There is no cooking involved in this lovely little recipe. So when the temperature soars in summer and the thought of turning on the oven reduces you to a melting puddle, fear not! This is one recipe you can whip up just using your trusty food processor.

To make the brownie, pulse the pecans into a powder in your food processor. Add the remaining ingredients and process until it all starts sticking together. Line a 20 × 30 cm (8 × 12 in) baking tin with baking parchment. Press half of the brownie mixture evenly into the tin, either with your hands or the back of a spoon. This will be the bottom half of your sandwiches.

To make the avocado nice cream, blend the bananas, avocados, lemon juice, vanilla extract, salt and honey in a high speed blender or food processor for 1 minute, until smooth, creamy and the consistency of soft-serve ice cream.

Spread the nice cream onto the brownie layer then put the tin in the freezer for a few hours until the nice cream has firmed up. Press the remaining half of the brownie mixture on top of the nice cream layer, then return to the freezer for at least two hours, to firm up.

To make the chocolate shell, simply whisk all the ingredients together until smooth. Pour the chocolate shell mix into a tall glass (this will make dipping the sandwiches much easier).

Take the tin out of the freezer and lift the brownie and nice-cream sandwich out onto a chopping board. Cut into slices and then dip each slice into the chocolate coating. Pop the coated slices on a tray lined with parchment, then put into the freezer for one last time so that the chocolate hardens. Before serving, let them thaw for 10–15 minutes.

These are best eaten within a couple of days, although they will keep for up to a couple of weeks. Wrap them well in cling film (plastic wrap) to keep the ice crystals away and to ensure the avocado stays green.

PUDDINGS

FROZEN BERRIES WITH MATCHA NICE CREAM AND HOT WHITE CHOCOLATE SAUCE

Serves 2

For the matcha nice cream:
3 tbsp tinned coconut milk, chilled (thick part only)
1 tbsp matcha powder • 3 bananas, peeled and frozen
1 tbsp honey • ½ ripe avocado • 2 tbsp light olive oil

For the hot white chocolate sauce:
150 g (5 oz/1 cup) white chocolate, broken into small pieces
3 tbsp coconut cream, chilled (thick part only)

200 g (7 oz) mixed frozen berries, to serve

❋

Hands-down, this has to be one of my favourite puddings. Frozen berries served straight as they are with hot white chocolate sauce poured over them so they start to melt. All of this enhanced by the matcha green tea-flavoured nice cream. Too dreamy for words.

To make the matcha nice cream, scoop the coconut milk into a small bowl and add the matcha powder. Whisk well to fully combine and form a paste. Put the bananas into a food processor and pulse to break them down into smaller pieces. Add the honey, avocado, oil and matcha paste and continue to blend until thick and creamy, scraping down the sides every 30 seconds. Process until the mixture becomes completely smooth and the consistency of soft-serve ice cream.

You can eat the nice cream right away while it has a soft-serve consistency or place into a freezer-proof container and freeze for a couple of hours until solid. Allow the nice cream to soften for 10–15 minutes before scooping like traditional ice cream.

To make the sauce, melt the white chocolate and coconut cream in a heatproof bowl suspended over a pan that's half-full of simmering water. Stir the chocolate until smooth. Take care not to overheat the sauce, or the chocolate will seize into a hard lump. Remove from the heat.

To serve, scatter the frozen berries on plates or in shallow bowls. Scoop on the ice cream and then drizzle the hot chocolate sauce over the top and serve immediately.

CINNAMON-BAKED APPLES WITH BANANA BREAD NICE CREAM

Serves 4

For the banana bread nice cream:
3 large ripe bananas, peeled and frozen
60 g (2 oz/½ cup) cashews, soaked for 4–6 hours, then drained
1½ tbsp rum • ½ tbsp coconut sugar • ½ tsp vanilla extract
½ tsp ground cinnamon • a pinch of salt • 60 g (2 oz/½ cup) cacao butter
60 g (2 oz/½ cup) chopped roasted walnuts

For the baked apples:
4 green apples • 4 tbsp coconut sugar • 4 tbsp maple syrup
4 tbsp vegan butter or coconut oil
2 tsp ground cinnamon

A cooling dollop of banana bread nice cream on top of a coconut sugar baked apple is an insanely good combo. This banana bread nice cream is a nod to all the delicious flavours you get within a great banana bread and it just goes so well with the baked apples.

To make the nice cream, blitz the bananas and cashews in a food processor or blender until completely smooth, scraping down the sides every 30 seconds, if necessary. Add the rum, coconut sugar, vanilla extract, cinnamon, salt and cacao butter, and blend again to incorporate. Spoon the mixture into a freezer-proof container and stir through the chopped walnuts. Freeze for 2–3 hours to firm up. Allow to thaw for 10 minutes before serving.

To make the baked apples, preheat the oven to 170°C (340°F/Gas 3). Scoop out the core from the top of the apples, leaving a well. Do not cut all the way through. Stuff each apple with 1 tablespoon coconut sugar and maple syrup. Place a small piece of butter or coconut oil on top, then place in a shallow baking dish and sprinkle with the cinnamon.

Bake in the oven for 15 minutes, until the sugar begins to caramelise and the apples are tender when you pierce them with a knife. You want them lovely and soft but not collapsing and mushy. Serve each baked apple immedietely with a scoop of the banana bread nice cream.

GINGERY POACHED RHUBARB WITH COCONUT NICE CREAM AND GINGERBREAD CRUMBLE

Serves 4

For the gingerbread crumble:
80 g (3 oz/¼ cup) cashews • 40 g (1½ oz/¼ cup) Medjool dates, pitted and roughly chopped
¼ tsp ground ginger • ¼ tsp ground cinnamon (or more to taste)
¼ tsp grated or ground nutmeg • 2 large pinches of Himalayan crystal salt or sea salt

For the rhubarb:
4 rhubarb stalks, chopped into 5 cm (2 in) pieces
zest and juice of 1 orange • 1 tsp vanilla extract • 1.5 cm (½ in) grated ginger • 2 tsp honey

For the coconut nice cream:
4 bananas, peeled and frozen • 4 tbsp coconut milk, chilled (thick part only)
4 tbsp desiccated coconut • 60 ml (2 fl oz) coconut oil, melted
1 tbsp maple syrup

This is such a deliciously pretty dish – the flavour combination of rhubarb, coconut, orange and ginger is a real triumph. The gingerbread crumble will stay fresh for up to 2 weeks, stored in an airtight container in the fridge. It's delicious sprinkled on top of fresh fruit, smoothie bowls or nice cream, of course.

To make the crumble, put the cashews into a food processor and process until coarsely ground. Add the dates, spices and salt. Process again until well combined. Set aside.

For the rhubarb, put all the ingredients in a heavy-based pan with a lid. Bring to the boil, then turn off the heat and leave to sit with the lid on. The rhubarb should be lovely and soft. Leave to cool to room temperature.

Make the coconut nice cream by simply blending the ingredients in a food processor until thick, creamy, and smooth, scraping down the sides every 30 seconds. To serve, spoon the coconut nice cream into little cups, top with the poached rhubarb and scatter over the gingerbread crumble.

Top Tip: For a choco-coconut Bounty paradise experience, stir through some chopped chocolate.

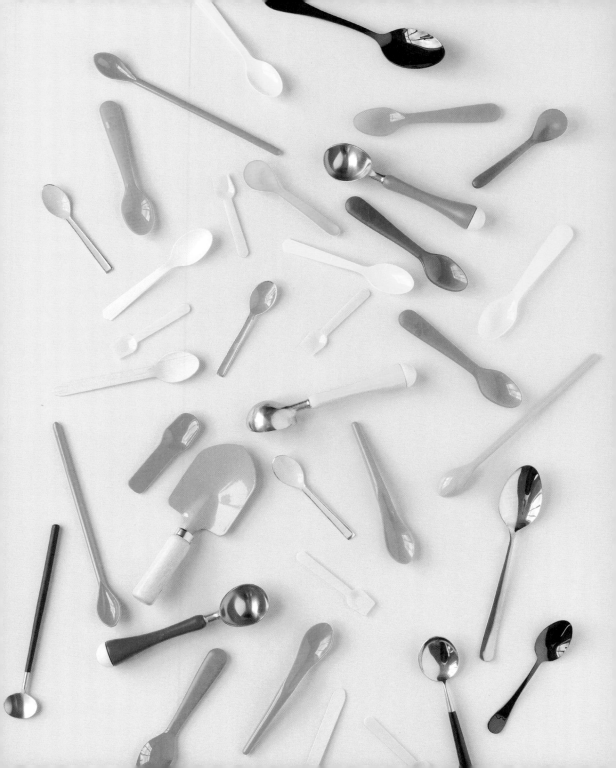

BANANA SPLIT BAKE WITH CANDIED PECANS

Serves 4

For the candied pecans:
50 ml (2 fl oz/1¼ cup) maple syrup • 1 tbsp coconut oil
1 tsp ground cinnamon • 100 g (3½ oz/¾ cup) pecans

For the banana split bake:
4 large bananas, peeled and halved lengthways
2 tbsp coconut oil • 2 tbsp coconut sugar

For the choco-chip nice cream:
80 g (3 oz/½ cup) cashews, soaked in water overnight, (or for at least 4 hours) until soft
1 tbsp maple syrup • 60 ml (2 fl oz) almond milk
4 bananas, peeled and frozen • 100 g (3½ oz/⅔ cup) dark chocolate chips

Toppings:
4 tbsp Raspberry Mint Coulis (page 129)
4 tbsp melted peanut butter
1 handful of fresh raspberries

❋

This pudding is a bit of a delicious show-stopper but it's lovely and simple to put together. Serve it straight from the oven to the table, hand around the forks, top with nice cream and allow everyone to just dig in. Elbows at the ready...

To make the candied pecans, preheat the oven to 200°C (400°F/Gas 6). Heat the maple syrup, coconut oil and cinnamon in a saucepan over low heat. Stir gently to combine and until the coconut oil has melted.

Line a 20 × 20 cm (8 × 8in) baking tray with parchment paper and spread the pecans over the paper. Pour the mixture onto the nuts. Toast for about 10 minutes, until they're golden brown but not burnt. (You may want to stir the mix once during this time to prevent the nuts from catching.) When they are done, leave to cool completely.

continue overleaf

To make the banana split bake, increase the oven temperature to 220°C (430°F/Gas 7). Arrange the bananas, cut side up, in a 3 cm (1¼ in) deep, 19 × 30 cm (7½ × 12 in) baking tray.

Melt the coconut oil and coconut sugar in a saucepan over medium heat, stirring until smooth. Pour this mixture over the bananas. Bake for 12–15 minutes, or until golden. You can baste the bananas halfway through with the delicious coconutty liquid. Remove and set aside to cool for 5 minutes.

For the choco-chip nice cream, drain and rinse the cashews and put them in a blender or food processor with the maple syrup and almond milk. Blend until creamy and smooth, then add the frozen bananas, and blend again. Once thick and creamy, stir through the chopped chocolate chips. Spoon the mixture into a freezer-proof container and freeze for 2–3 hours to firm up. Allow to thaw for 10 minutes before serving.

Serve in the tray you cooked the bananas in, topped with scoops of choco-chip nice cream. Drizzle with the Raspberry Mint Coulis, melted peanut butter and fresh raspberries. Sprinkle with the candied pecan rubble.

AFFOGATO WITH CHOCOLATE-COATED COFFEE BEANS

✤

Serves 2

4 bananas, peeled and frozen • ½ tsp ground cinnamon
Easy Chocolate Sauce (page 133) • 1 shot espresso or strong coffee

For the chocolate-covered coffee beans:
85 g (3 oz/½ cup) dark chocolate chips or chocolate chunks
85 g (3 oz/1 cup) coffee beans
cocoa powder, for dusting (optional)

✤

Get your caffeine fix with this dairy-free version of the classic Italian dessert. To make it extra special, add a drizzle of chocolate syrup and some chocolate-coated coffee beans for a bit of a crunch.

To make the chocolate-covered beans, melt the chocolate in a heatproof bowl suspended over a pan that's half-full of simmering water. Stir the chocolate until smooth.

Put roughly a third of the coffee beans in the melted chocolate. Stir around until coated. Remove your coated coffee beans from the chocolate using a fork and place on a sheet of parchment paper, but don't allow the coated beans to touch each other. Continue coating your coffee beans until all are finished. If you like, take them one step further and roll your chocolate-covered coffee beans in cocoa powder before they harden.

Let the chocolate-covered beans harden overnight in an airtight container. If you are in a hurry, put them in the freezer (spread out on a tray) for 30 minutes.

When you are ready to eat the affogato, blitz the bananas and cinnamon in a blender or food processor until thick and creamy, scraping down the sides every 30 seconds. Process until the mixture becomes completely smooth and the consistency of soft-serve ice cream.

Scoop the nice cream between bowls or cups, drizzle some chocolate sauce on top and then pour a shot of espresso over the top. To finish, scatter with chocolate-covered coffee beans.

FOIL-BAKED BANANA SPLITS WITH MAPLE PECAN SOFT-SERVE NICE CREAM

Serves 4

*4 bananas • 4 tbsp roughly chopped dark chocolate
4 tbsp desiccated coconut • 4 tbsp maple syrup*

For the maple pecan soft-serve nice cream:
*4 large bananas, peeled and frozen • ¼ tsp vanilla powder or extract
a large pinch of Himalayan crystal salt or sea salt
1½ tbsp maple syrup • 30 g (1 oz/¼ cup) toasted pecans, crushed
60 ml (2 fl oz) almond milk*

Toppings:
*chopped pecans • blueberries • nut butters • ground cinnamon
coconut oil • desiccated coconut • dried cranberries • strawberries*

I love serving these still wrapped in their foil parcels, so that each person can unwrap their own little pudding, and then add a scoop of the maple pecan nice cream at the table. You can really play around with the toppings and create some fun alternatives.

Preheat the oven to 180°C (350°F/Gas 4).

Take the bananas and, with the skins still on, slice them down the middle. Fill each banana with a tablespoon of chocolate and desiccated coconut, then drizzle with the maple syrup. Wrap the bananas separately in foil, put on a baking tray and bake for 8–10 minutes. To check whether they are done, carefully peek inside one of the parcels – the banana should be soft but not mushy. Remove from the oven and set aside.

To make the maple pecan nice cream, put the ingredients in a food processor and blend until thick and creamy, scraping down the sides every 30 seconds. Process until the mixture becomes completely smooth and the consistency of soft-serve ice cream.

Let everyone carefully (it will be piping hot!) open their own parcels and top with a dollop of the maple pecan nice cream and their choice of toppings.

BANOFFEE NICE-CREAM TART

Serves 10

For the crust:
120 g (4 oz/¾ cup) Brazil nuts (macadamia, almond or pecan would work too)
25 g (1 oz/¼ cup) almond meal (ground almond) • 25 g (1 oz/¼ cup) buckwheat flour
60 ml (2 fl oz) coconut oil, melted • 2 tbsp maple syrup

For the salted caramel layer:
125 g (4½ oz/½ cup) almond butter or other nut butter
60 g (2 oz/¼ cup) coconut cream • 125 ml (4 fl oz) maple syrup
1 tsp ground cinnamon (optional) • ½ tsp vanilla extract (optional) • a pinch of flaked sea salt

For the chocolate maple nice cream:
5 bananas, peeled and frozen • 400 ml (13 fl oz) almond milk
1 heaped tbsp unsweetened cacao powder or cocoa powder
1 tbsp of maple syrup, to taste

Toppings:
2 fresh bananas, sliced • Whipped Coconut Cream (page 141) • grated dark chocolate

This tart is gorgeous. All the deliciousness of a banoffee pie but a little bit more special.

Place the ingredients for the crust into a food processor and pulse until the mixture resembles rubbly wet sand. Tip into a 20 cm (8 in) tart tin and press to form an even layer, pressing the mixture into the sides. Pop into the fridge for 30 minutes to firm up.

For the salted caramel layer, simply mix everything together in a bowl. It should be gorgeous and thick. Now spoon into the chilled tart case, spreading the mixture evenly over the surface. If serving straight away move onto the steps below, otherwise return the tart to the fridge until ready to serve. It will keep happily like this for a good few days.

When almost ready to serve, put the ingredients for the chocolate maple nice cream into a blender or food processor and blend until thick and creamy, scraping down the sides every 30 seconds. Process until the mixture becomes completely smooth and has the consistency of soft-serve ice cream. Spread the nice cream on top of the caramel in the tart case. Then arrange the banana slices on top and finish with whipped coconut cream and some grated dark chocolate.

PEANUT BUTTER AND CHOCOLATE TART

❁

Serves 10

For the chocolate tart crust:
200 g (7 oz/2 cups) ground almonds (almond meal)
40 g (1½ oz/⅓ cup) unsweetened cacao powder or cocoa powder • 1 tbsp coconut flour
a pinch of salt • 5 tbsp melted coconut oil • 80 ml (2½ fl oz) maple syrup

For the peanut butter filling:
5 bananas, peeled and frozen • 400 ml (13½ fl oz) almond milk
4 tbsp smooth peanut butter • 1 tbsp maple syrup • 125 ml (4 fl oz) coconut milk, chilled

For the chocolate topping:
4 tbsp melted coconut oil • 60 ml (2 fl oz) melted cacao butter
4 tbsp unsweetened cacao powder or cocoa powder • 3 tbsp maple syrup

For the topping:
2 tbsp peanut butter, melted
75 g (2½ oz/½ cup) crushed peanuts • sprinkling of sea salt

❁

Peanut butter, banana and chocolate are just meant to be eaten together. The baked dark chocolate crust contrasts beautifully with the smooth and creamy peanut centre. Delicious!

Preheat the oven to 180°C (350°F/Gas 5) and lightly grease a 20 cm (8 in) tart tin. To make the crust, combine the dry ingredients in a large bowl. Whisk the coconut oil and maple syrup in a separate bowl then pour into the dry ingredients. Use your hands to form the mixture into a dough, and pop it in the centre of the tart tin. Press the dough into an even layer, making sure to go up the sides. Use a fork to poke the surface with a few holes, and bake for 12 minutes or until the top begins to turn brown. Remove the crust from the oven and set aside on a wire rack to cool completely.

To make the filling, blend all the ingredients in a food processor until smooth and creamy. Spoon into the chocolate tart case and pop into the freezer while you prepare the chocolate topping.

For the chocolate topping, combine the ingredients in a bowl, and then pour on top of the tart.

Drizzle over the melted peanut butter and sprinkle some crushed peanuts and sea salt on top. Freeze for another 2 hours (or up to 3 days). Before serving, let the tart soften a little out of the freezer for 20–25 minutes.

SAUCES AND TOPPINGS

THREE INGREDIENT SALTED CARAMEL SAUCE

❋

Makes approx. 240 ml (8 fl oz)

170 ml (5½ fl oz) coconut nectar or maple syrup
65 g (2 oz/¼ cup) almond butter, plus 2 tbsp extra
¼ tsp sea salt

❋

This is such a delicious and easy version of a salted caramel sauce without all the butter and refined sugar. Great for drizzling and dipping.

Simply mix the ingredients together until well combined. Store in an airtight container and keep it in the fridge until ready to use. The sauce will thicken over time. It will keep for up to a week.

CARAMEL SWIRL

❋

Makes approx. 360 ml (12 fl oz)

175 g (6 oz/1 cup) Medjool dates
2 tbsp almond butter • 3 tbsp maple syrup • 1 tsp vanilla extract
¼ tsp sea salt • 2 tbsp water

❋

This thick caramel swirl is delicious spooned straight from the jar. But its also great stirred through a nice cream before you freeze it. You can use ordinary dates instead of Medjool dates – just soak them in warm water for 30 minutes first, then drain.

First remove the stones from the dates. Then add everything to a food processor until thick and creamy. You may need to stop and scrape down the sides to encourage everything to blend together properly. Store in a sealed jar in the fridge. It will keep for up to a week.

DATE SYRUP

Makes approx. 600 ml (20 fl oz)

400 g (14 oz/2½ cups) dates, pitted
800 ml (28 fl oz) water

This is such a versatile syrup. It's great used as a sweetener in recipes but it's also lovely as a sauce drizzled on top of your favourite nice cream.

Place the dates and water in a saucepan and bring to the boil. Reduce to a low simmer and cook for 2 hours or until the dates are very soft. If it begins to look dry, add a little more hot water. By the end of cooking, the mixture should be thick and caramel in colour. Leave to cool and then pour through cheesecloth into a large mixing bowl. Give the dates a really good squeeze, trying to get out as much of the liquid as possible.

Pour the strained liquid into a saucepan and simmer for another 20–30 minutes or until it has the consistency of maple syrup. Once cool, store in a sealed jar, in the fridge. It will keep for up to a week.

RASPBERRY MINT COULIS

Makes approx. 240 ml (8 fl oz)

125 g (4½ oz/1 cup) raspberries, fresh or frozen
1½ tbsp maple syrup • sprig of mint, leaves only

Such a simple but lovely thing to whip up. Swirl it through or drizzle it on pretty much anything for a burst of flavour.

Pop the raspberries and maple syrup into a blender or food processor and blitz until smooth. Add the fresh mint and blend again for a few seconds, adding a splash or two of water to get the desired consistency. Store in a sealed jar in the fridge. It will keep in the fridge for 2–3 days.

IT'S NOT NUTELLA® SPREAD

❋

Makes approx. 360 ml (12 fl oz)

135 g (5 oz/1 cup) hazelnuts, skinned
120 g (4½ oz/¾ cup) dark chocolate chips
185 ml (6 fl oz) almond milk
1½ tbsp mild honey or maple syrup
a pinch of sea salt

❋

Once you make your own Nutella®, there is no going back. It's simple, delicious and contains nothing but goodness.

Preheat the oven to 180°C (350°F/Gas 4). Evenly spread the hazelnuts on a baking sheet and roast for about 15 minutes. Remove and wrap the hot hazelnuts in a clean tea towel and allow to cool 10 minutes. Remove the skins by rubbing the hazelnuts with the tea towel.

In a saucepan, melt the chocolate chips, almond milk, honey and salt over low heat. Remove from the heat once the chocolate has completely melted, and allow to cool slightly while you get on with the hazelnuts.

Put the hazelnuts in a food processor and pulse for about 5 minutes until they form a butter-like consistency, scraping the sides of the processor every 30 seconds. Add the chocolate mixture and pulse until well combined and smooth.

Transfer the spread to a glass jar, allow to cool completely, then screw on the lid and pop in the fridge where it will thicken. It will keep for a good couple of weeks.

THE ULTIMATE BUTTERSCOTCH CARAMEL SAUCE

✻

Makes approx. 360 ml (12 fl oz)

175 g (6 oz/1 cup) Medjool dates · 40 g (1½ oz/¼ cup) cashews
250 ml (8½ fl oz) almond milk · 1 tsp vanilla extract
1 tbsp coconut oil · ½ tsp sea salt

✻

This really is the ultimate butterscotch caramel sauce using no refined sugars. Absolutely delicious drizzled on just about anything, from nice cream cakes to waffles, or just eaten straight off the spoon.

Remove the stones from the dates. Meanwhile, soak cashews in a bowl of freshly boiled water and leave for 30 minutes, then drain the water.

Add the dates and cashews to a blender with the remaining ingredients, and blend until smooth and creamy. This keeps happily in the fridge in an airtight container for up to a week.

CHOCOLATE SAUCES

These two chocolate sauces are really easy to make and are great to have in your repertoire. Both sauces are best served on the same day you make them, but will last for up to a week, if kept in the fridge. You may need to reblitz them first, and reheat on a gentle heat.

EASY CHOCOLATE SAUCE

✽

Makes approx. 240 ml (8 fl oz)

60 g (2 oz/⅓ cup) pitted Medjool dates · 125 ml (4 fl oz) almond milk or milk of choice
15 g (½ oz) dark chocolate or 1½ tbsp cacao or cocoa powder
a pinch of flaked sea salt · 1 tsp vanilla extract

✽

Put the dates and almond milk into a blender or food processor, and blitz until smooth. Pour into a saucepan and bring to the boil. Reduce the heat to a simmer, continue to cook, stirring over a low flame for 5–10 minutes, until thickened. Remove from the heat and stir in the chocolate or cacao until well combined. Add the sea salt and vanilla extract and serve warm. This is best served immediately, but can keep in the fridge for up to a week (but reheat it on a gentle heat).

DAIRY-FREE WHITE CHOCOLATE SAUCE

✽

Makes approx. 360 ml (12 fl oz)

220 g (8 oz/1 cup) cacao butter
120 g (4½ oz/1 cup) raw macadamia nuts, roughly chopped
60 ml (2 fl oz) coconut nectar or agave syrup
1 tbsp tinned coconut milk, chilled (thick part only), plus extra if needed

✽

Simply blitz everything together in a food processor. Add a little more coconut milk if you need it runnier. Best served instantly, as a lovely glaze, but can keep for up to a month in the fridge.

HONEY AND QUINOA GRANOLA

❋

Serves 6

260 g (9 oz/¾ cup) honey • 125 ml (4 fl oz) coconut oil, melted
1 tsp ground cinnamon • a pinch of sea salt
1 tsp vanilla extract • 300 g (10½ oz/3 cups) rolled oats
100 g (3½ oz/½ cup) raw quinoa, rinsed well in cold water and drained
300 g (10½ oz/2 cups) raw almonds, roughly chopped
30 g (1 oz/½ cup) sweetened coconut flakes
1–2 cups dried fruits (optional)

❋

This granola is so light and moreish that you're in danger of eating the whole lot in one go!

Preheat the oven to 190°C (375°F/Gas 5). Line a large rimmed baking tray with parchment paper.

In a small saucepan, heat the honey, coconut oil, cinnamon and salt over low heat, stirring occasionally until melted and thoroughly combined. Remove from the heat. Stir in the vanilla extract, then set aside.

In a large bowl, stir together the oats, quinoa, almonds, and coconut flakes. Pour the wet ingredients over the oaty mixture and stir until well combined. Tip the granola onto the prepared baking sheet and bake for 35–45 minutes, or until golden brown and fragrant. Stir the granola halfway through cooking.

Remove from the oven and leave to cool completely. Break into bite-sized chunks and then stir in the dried fruit, if using. This keeps well in an airtight container at room temperature for several days. Serve with a dollop of my Raspberry Ripple Coconut Nice Cream on page 40.

COCONUT, CHERRY AND BUCKWHEAT GRANOLA

Serves 6

200 g (7 oz/2 cups) rolled oats (not quick-cook variety)
150 g (5 oz/1 cup) brown rice flakes • 168 g (6 oz/1 cup) buckwheat groats
1 tsp ground cinnamon • a pinch of sea salt • 80 ml (2½ fl oz) maple syrup
3 tbsp vegetable oil or melted coconut oil • 1 tsp vanilla extract
1 handful of dried cherries • 1 handful of hazelnuts or almonds, chopped
1 handful of unsweetened coconut flakes

This granola is so easy to make and packed full of flavour. Serve in a bowl with scoops of the Mango and Passion Fruit Nice Cream on page 40, for an extra special breakfast treat!

First, make the granola. Preheat the oven to 150°C (300°F/Gas 4). Line a baking sheet with parchment paper. In a large bowl, combine the oats, brown rice flakes, buckwheat groats, cinnamon and salt. In another bowl, combine the maple syrup, oil and vanilla extract. Pour the wet ingredients into the dry and mix well. Tip the mixture onto the baking sheet and spread out evenly, in one layer.

Bake in the oven for 30 minutes, stirring about every 10 minutes or so to keep it from burning. Remove and add the cherries, hazelnuts and coconut flakes. Continue to bake for an additional 10–15 minutes. When the granola sounds 'crispy' it's done.

Remove from the oven and let is rest for about 15 minutes. Do not stir. While resting, the granola will have a chance to stick together and clump up. When completely cool, store in an airtight container. It will keep for a good couple of weeks.

EDIBLE GRANOLA
BERRY BOWLS

❋

Make about 18 bowls

coconut or olive oil, for greasing • 300 g (10½ oz/3 cups) rolled oats
115 (4 oz/1 cup) pecans, chopped • 125 ml (4 fl oz) maple syrup
100 g (3 ½ oz/½ cup) coconut sugar • 200 g (7 oz/1 cup) freeze-dried strawberries
½ cup desiccated coconut • ½ cup water

❋

There is something wonderfully satisfying about an edible bowl. These flapjack bowls have little bursts of berries and provide a welcome coconut crunch to any nice cream. Of course you can bake these in a tray for normal flapjacks too.

Preheat the oven to 180°C (350°F/Gas 4). Grease a muffin tin (or two tins if necessary) with coconut or olive oil.

Combine all the ingredients together in a mixing bowl. Spoon the mixture into the holes in the muffin tin, and then use the back of a spoon (or your fingers) to press the oat mixture into the base of the hole and up the sides. You don't want the layer to be too thick, about 2 mm (⅛ in) is perfect.

Bake for 20–25 minutes or until golden and crispy. Remove and let them cool for 10 minutes before carefully popping the granola bowls out of the muffin tin to cool completely on a wire rack. I love to serve this with scoops of my Vanilla Nice Cream with Raspberries on page 22.

CARAMEL POPCORN

Serves 4–6

4 tbsp coconut oil • 200 g (7 oz/1 cup) corn kernels
125 ml (4 fl oz) agave syrup • 250 ml (8½ fl oz) tinned coconut milk, chilled (thick part only)
2 tsp vanilla extract • ¼ tsp sea salt

Dangerously moreish, this caramel popcorn is a breeze to make. Surprisingly, it also keeps wonderfully well in the freezer, so it can always be on standby. Phew.

Heat a large stainless-steel pan with a lid over medium-high heat until hot. Add the coconut oil along with two corn kernels and close the lid. Once you hear the corn kernels popping, it means the oil is hot enough.

Open the lid and add the corn kernels. Secure the lid and start to shake the pan as the corn starts to pop, and increase to more vigorous shaking as the popping speeds up. When the popping slows down to more than 10 seconds between each pop, remove the pan from heat and transfer the popcorn to a large bowl. Set aside.

Return the pan to a medium-high heat, discarding any unpopped or burnt kernels and wipe clean a with paper towel if necessary. Add the agave syrup, bring to the boil and let it cook for 2–3 minutes; the agave will darken to make a good caramel sauce.

Add the coconut milk, vanilla extract and salt, and stir to combine. Bring to the boil, reduce the heat to medium-low and let the caramel sauce cook for 20–25 minutes, stirring occassionally, until thickened and a shade darker.

When it's ready, immediately drizzle the hot caramel sauce over your popcorn and gently mix with a spatula to distribute it evenly. (I like to drizzle some caramel and mix, then drizzle again and mix.)

Line a baking sheet or cooling rack with parchment paper and transfer the caramel popcorn to it. Freeze for 10 minutes. Remove from the freezer and break into smaller pieces.

This can be eaten straight away or stored in an airtight container in the freezer for up to 3 months.

WHIPPED COCONUT CREAM

✱

Makes 240 ml (8 fl oz)

250 ml (8½ fl oz) coconut cream, chilled (thick part only)
a drop of vanilla extract · a drizzle of maple syrup

✱

Whipped coconut cream is a wonder. Once made, you'll wonder how you ever managed without it. It's dreamy atop sundaes, or spooned over tarts. And try it with a little cacao powder for an instant chocolate mousse. This is one of those lovely recipes where a recipe isn't strictly necessary once you grasp the concept.

Scoop the thick coconut cream into a bowl and then whisk well. Add a splash of vanilla extract and a squeeze of maple syrup. Whisk for another couple of seconds until it is creamy and smooth. Store in an airtight container and keep in the fridge for 4–5 days.

MAPLE COCONUT CHIPS

✱

Makes 480 ml (16 oz)

60 ml (2 fl oz) maple syrup
110 g (4 oz/2 cups) raw (dehydrated) unsweetened coconut chips
a pinch of sea salt

✱

Simple yet delicious, these are sensational sprinkled on top of your favourite nice cream.

Preheat the oven to 190°C (375°F/Gas 5). Line a baking sheet with parchment paper. In a bowl, gently toss all of the ingredients. Spread evenly on the baking sheet and toast in the oven for 15-20 minutes, stirring every 5 minutes until the coconut is golden brown. Store in an airtight container and store in a cool, dark place for a few days.

EDIBLE CHOCOLATE BOWLS

❋

Makes 4

300 g (10½ oz) chocolate of choice, broken into small pieces
50 g (1¾ oz/½ cup) hazelnuts, very finely chopped
4 small balloons

❋ ·

People are always really impressed by these, which (let's be honest) is always nice.

Melt the chocolate in a heatproof bowl suspended over a pan that's half-full of simmering water. Stir the chocolate until smooth. Remove from the heat and leave to cool for 5 minutes. Pour into a shallow bowl to make it easier to dip.

Blow up your balloons – you want each bowl to be about 10 cm (4 in) wide, so try to pick small balloons and don't blow them up too much. Tie with a knot.

Line a baking tray with parchment paper. Spread the chopped hazelnuts onto a plate. Holding the knotted end of the balloon, dip it into the melted chocolate to create your bowl shape.

Dip the balloon immediately into the chopped hazelnuts and then stand it on the lined tray and hold for a few seconds, until the chocolate pools around the base allowing you to let go of the balloon. Continue with the remaining balloons. Chill the balloons for at least 30 minutes in the fridge or if you're in a hurry pop them into the freezer until set.

When the chocolate has set, pop the balloons and carefully peel them away from the bowls. Keep in the fridge until ready to use.

Top Tip: Feel free to play around with the toppings. Freeze-dried raspberries, desiccated coconut or toasted flaked almonds all work well.

GLUTEN-FREE, DAIRY-FREE BUT DELICIOUS NICE-CREAM CONES

❋

Makes 6

3 large eggs • 150 g (5 ½ oz/¾ cup) coconut sugar • 130 ml (4½ fl oz) vegetable oil
1 tsp vanilla extract • 260 g (9 oz/1¾ cups) gluten-free plain (all-purpose) flour or normal flour
2 tsp baking powder • ½ tsp ground cinnamon

❋

These are well worth the effort because they taste so good. You will find the first few tries might be a bit trial and error, but it's always delicious eating the errors. I love to dip the tops of the cones in a chocolate-nutty sauce (you can use the same recipe as the Edible Chocolate Bowls on page 143).

In a bowl, whisk the eggs and coconut sugar until pale yellow and frothy. Stir in the oil, vanilla extract and 60 ml (2 fl oz) of water. In a separate bowl, whisk together the remaining ingredients then carefully fold in the wet ingredients together, being careful not to overmix.

Preheat a waffle cone maker and set the dial to about level 4 (or according to the manufacturer's instructions). Spoon about 2 tablespoons of the batter into the centre of the waffle iron and close. Cook for 1 minute, until golden. Working quickly, slide the waffle onto a clean tea towel and roll into a cone shape. Pinch the bottom together into a point and keep holding it in shape until it cools. Pop into a tumbler glass to help it maintain its cone shape as it cools. Repeat with the remaining batter.

Leave the cones to cool completely, then store in an airtight container for a few days at most but definitely best eaten on the day they are made.

Top Tip: If you want to make a little basket rather than a cone, lay the cooked waffle over an upturned large muffin tray and use your hands to help shape it as it cools. If you don't have a waffle cone maker, lightly grease a 15 cm (6 in) non-stick frying pan (skillet) on a medium-low heat. Add two tablespoons of the mixture and swirl the pan around to make an even, round, thin layer of batter. Cook for 1–2 minutes on both sides, until nice and golden. Slide onto a clean tea towel and roll into a cone, as above.

ABOUT THE AUTHOR

Margie Broadhead is a professional chef who trained at Ireland's world-renowned Ballymaloe Cookery School. She has worked in a number of top London restaurants, has cooked at Windsor Castle, as well as volunteering to teach Zulu women the art of cookery in South Africa.

Margie set up her catering company and hugely popular blog, *Made by Margie*. Margie's blog is a must for anyone with a love of food and is full of ideas for how to get creative in the kitchen, as well as showing that eating healthily is easier than you think (and far more delicious).

@madebymargie @nananicecream

ACKNOWLEDGEMENTS

It's looking increasingly more unlikely I will ever win an Oscar, so I'm going to take this opportunity to thank the people in my life for all their support.

This book has been a dream to write and there are obvious people I need to thank in addition to my friends and family for helping to bring it all to life. Thank you to my amazing photographer Jacqui Melville who is both wonderful and talented. Thank you to my Commissioning Editor, Kajal Mistry, for approaching me in the first place and seeing the potential in Nana Nice Cream and for what this book could be. Thank you to Lucy Cufflin for helping me on the shoot, and thank you to Stuart Hardie for the amazing design.

And last but not least, thank you to *you*, for getting this book! I hope you enjoy reading it as much as I loved writing it.

First published in 2017 by Hardie Grant Books

Hardie Grant Books (UK)
52–54 Southwark Street
London SE1 1UN
hardiegrant.co.uk

Hardie Grant Books (Australia)
Ground Floor, Building 1
658 Church Street
Melbourne, VIC 3121
hardiegrant.com.au

British Library Cataloguing-in-Publication Data. A catalogue record
for this book is available from the British Library.

ISBN: 978-1-78488-083-5

Publisher: Kate Pollard
Commissioning Editor: Kajal Mistry
Editorial Assistant: Hannah Roberts
Publishing Assistant: Eila Purvis
Cover and Internal Design: Stuart Hardie
Photography © Jacqui Melville
Styling: Margie Broadhead
Prop and Styling: Lucy Cufflin
Props: Ginger Whisk
Copy editor: Kate Wanwimolruk
Proofreader: Kay Halsey
Indexer: Cathy Heath
Colour Reproduction by p2d

Printed and bound in China by 1010

10 9 8 7 6 5 4 3 2 1